EVERYMAN,
I WILL GO WITH THEE
AND BE THY GUIDE,
IN THY MOST NEED
TO GO BY THY SIDE

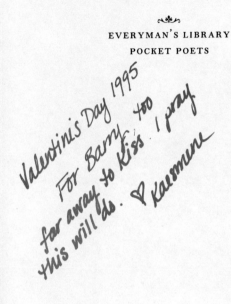

EVERYMAN'S LIBRARY
POCKET POETS

Valentine's Day 1995
For Barry, too
far away to kiss. I pray
this will do. ♡ Kaesmene

Love Poems

Selected and edited by
Peter Washington

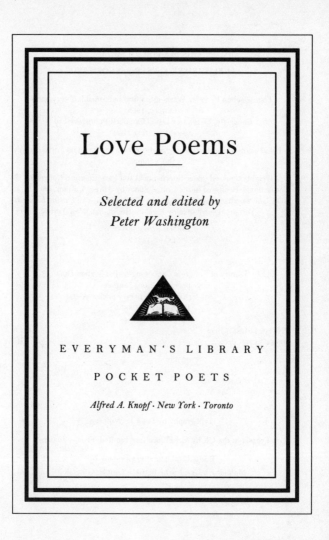

EVERYMAN'S LIBRARY

POCKET POETS

Alfred A. Knopf · New York · Toronto

THIS IS A BORZOI BOOK

PUBLISHED BY ALFRED A. KNOPF, INC.

This selection by Peter Washington first published in Everyman's
Library, 1993
Copyright © 1993 by David Campbell Publishers Ltd.
Second printing 1994

ISBN 0-679-42906-9
LC 93-11427

Library of Congress Cataloging-in-Publication Data
Love poems / various [authors].
p.   cm.—(Everyman's library pocket poets)
ISBN 0-679-42906-9
1. Poetry. I. Series.
PN6110.L6L49   1993   93-11427
808.81'9354—dc20   CIP

Typography by Peter B. Willberg

Typeset in the UK by MS Filmsetting Limited, Frome, Somerset

Printed and bound in Germany by
Mohndruck Graphische Betriebe GmbH, Gütersloh

CONTENTS

LOVE AND POETRY

PRAISING THE LOVED ONE

8

FIDELITY AND INCONSTANCY

9

ABSENCE, ESTRANGEMENT
AND PARTING

11

FOREWORD

My selection of poems for the anthology which follows has been guided by simple principles. Each piece had to be first-rate in its own way, and each had to contribute something distinctive to our understanding of love. Where there is similarity of mood, there is difference of emphasis; where there is repetition of an idea, there is variety in music. The juxtaposition of apparently comparable lyrics brings out their differences, and although the poems are arranged in broad categories which follow an obvious sequence, it is the echoes they set up in one another which enrich them all.

Inevitably, some poets are represented here more extensively than others, but I make no apology for giving what might seem to be disproportionate space to Donne and Marvell, Pasternak and Akhmatova, Rossetti and Graves. Though it may not be fashionable to say so, each articulates in an instantly recognizable voice a whole world of amorous experience which is both highly characteristic and yet universally accessible.

At the same time, it has been fascinating to approach my theme from sharply diverse perspectives: from ancient India and Greece, medieval Japan, renaissance England, nineteenth-century France and twentieth-century America (both north and south).

Choosing an anthology of poems is always a daunting experience, especially if the field of choice is as wide as it must be when the theme is love. So many people have written so well on the subject over so many centuries, that every poem presented here might be replaced several times over with English verse of equal quality. Opening up the selection process to other languages has immeasurably complicated my task, but has also immeasurably enriched it, and the great thrill of making this selection has been to discover marvellous poems previously unknown to me. I hope the results will bring the same excitement and pleasure to my readers.

PETER WASHINGTON

DEFINITIONS
AND
PERSUASIONS

THE REVELATION

An idle poet, here and there,
   Looks round him; but, for all the rest,
The world, unfathomably fair,
   Is duller than a witling's jest.
Love wakes men, once a lifetime each;
   They lift their heavy lids, and look;
And, lo, what one sweet page can teach,
   They read with joy, then shut the book.
And some give thanks, and some blaspheme
   And most forget; but, either way,
That and the Child's unheeded dream
Is all the light of all their day.

SYMPTOMS OF LOVE

Love is a universal migraine,
A bright stain on the vision
Blotting out reason.

Symptoms of true love
Are leanness, jealousy,
Laggard dawns;

Are omens and nightmares –
Listening for a knock,
Waiting for a sign:

For a touch of her fingers
In a darkened room,
For a searching look.

Take courage, lover!
Could you endure such grief
At any hand but hers?

18   ROBERT GRAVES (1895–1985)

THE DEFINITION OF LOVE

My Love is of a birth as rare
As 'tis for object strange and high:
It was begotten by Despair
Upon Impossibility.

Magnanimous Despair alone
Could show me so divine a thing,
Where feeble Hope could ne'er have flown
But vainly flapped its tinsel wing.

And yet I quickly might arrive
Where my extended soul is fixt,
But Fate does iron wedges drive,
And always crowds itself betwixt.

For Fate with jealous eye does see
Two perfect Loves; nor lets them close:
Their union would her ruin be,
And her tyrannic power depose.

And therefore her decrees of steel
Us as the distant poles have placed,
(Though Love's whole world on us doth wheel)
Not by themselves to be embraced.

Unless the giddy heaven fall,
And earth some new convulsion tear;
And, us to join, the world should all
Be cramped into a planisphere.

As lines so Loves oblique may well
Themselves in every angle greet:
But ours so truly parallel,
Though infinite, can never meet.

Therefore the Love which us doth bind
But Fate so enviously debars,
Is the conjunction of the mind,
And opposition of the stars.

20   ANDREW MARVELL (1621—1678)

IN LOVE FOR LONG

I've been in love for long
With what I cannot tell
And will contrive a song
For the intangible
That has no mould or shape,
From which there's no escape.

It is not even a name,
Yet is all constancy;
Tried or untried, the same,
It cannot part from me;
A breath, yet as still
As the established hill.

It is not any thing,
And yet all being is;
Being, being, being,
Its burden and its bliss.
How can I ever prove
What it is I love?

This happy happy love
Is sieged with crying sorrows,
Crushed beneath and above
Between todays and morrows;
A little paradise
Held in the world's vice.

And there it is content
And careless as a child,
And in imprisonment
Flourishes sweet and wild;
In wrong, beyond wrong,
All the world's day long.

This love a moment known
For what I do not know
And in a moment gone
Is like the happy doe
That keeps its perfect laws
Between the tiger's paws
And vindicates its cause.

THE ANNIVERSARY

All Kings, and all their favourites,
    All glory of honours, beauties, wits,
The sun itself, which makes times, as they pass,
Is elder by a year now than it was
When thou and I first one another saw:
All other things to their destruction draw,
    Only our love hath no decay;
This no tomorrow hath, nor yesterday,
Running it never runs from us away,
But truly keeps his first, last, everlasting day.

Two graves must hide thine and my corse;
    If one might, death were no divorce.
Alas, as well as other Princes, we
(Who Prince enough in one another be)
Must leave at last in death these eyes and ears,
Oft fed with true oaths, and with sweet salt tears;
    But souls where nothing dwells but love
(All other thoughts being inmates) then shall prove
This, or a love increasèd there above,
When bodies to their graves, souls from their graves
    remove.

And then we shall be throughly blessed;
  But we no more than all the rest.
Here upon earth we're Kings, and none but we
Can be such Kings, nor of such subjects be;
Who is so safe as we? where none can do
Treason to us, except one of us two.
  True and false fears let us refrain,
Let us love nobly, and live, and add again
Years and years unto years, till we attain
To write threescore: this is the second of our reign.

LOVE IS NOT

Love is not just a function of the eyes.
Beautiful objects will, of course, inspire
Possessive urges – you need not despise
Your taste. But when insatiable desire
Inflames you for a girl who's out of fashion,
Lacking in glamour – plain, in fact – that fire
Is genuine; that's the authentic passion.
Beauty, though, any critic can admire.

MARCUS ARGENTARIUS (20 BC–30 AD),   25
TRANS. FLEUR ADCOCK (1934–   )

A DRINKING SONG

Wine comes in at the mouth
And love comes in at the eye;
That's all we know for truth
Before we grow old and die.
I lift the glass to my mouth,
I look at you, and I sigh.

WALSINGHAME

As you came from the holy land
    of Walsinghame
Met you not with my true love
    By the way as you came?

How shall I know your true love
    That have met many one
As I went to the holy land
    That have come, that have gone?

She is neither white nor brown
    But as the heavens fair
There is none hath a form so divine
    In the earth or the air.

Such an one did I meet, good Sir,
    Such an Angelic face,
Who like a queen, like a nymph, did appear
    By her gait, by her grace.

She hath left me here all alone,
    All alone as unknown,
Who sometimes did me lead with her self,
    And me loved as her own.

What's the cause that she leaves you alone
    And a new way doth take;
Who loved you once as her own
    And her joy did you make?

I have loved her all my youth,
    But now old, as you see,
Love likes not the falling fruit
    From the withered tree.

Know that love is a careless child
    And forgets promise past,
He is blind, he is deaf when he list
    And in faith never fast.

His desire is a dureless content
    And a trustless joy
He is won with a world of despair
    And is lost with a toy.

Of womenkind such indeed is the love
    Or the word Love abused
Under which many childish desires
    And conceits are excused.

But true Love is a durable fire
  In the mind ever burning;
Never sick, never old, never dead,
  From itself never turning.

LET ME NOT

Let me not to the marriage of true minds
Admit impediments, love is not love
Which alters when it alteration finds,
Or bends with the remover to remove.
O no! it is an ever-fixèd mark,
That looks on tempests and is never shaken;
It is the star to every wand'ring bark,
Whose worth's unknown, although his height be taken.
Love's not Time's fool, though rosy lips and cheeks
Within his bending sickle's compass come,
Love alters not with his brief hours and weeks,
But bears it out even to the edge of doom:
   If this be error and upon me proved,
   I never writ, nor no man ever loved.

THEY THAT HAVE POWER

They that have power to hurt, and will do none,
That do not do the thing, they most do show,
Who moving others, are themselves as stone,
Unmoved, cold, and to temptation slow:
They rightly do inherit heaven's graces,
And husband nature's riches from expense,
They are the Lords and owners of their faces,
Others, but stewards of their excellence:
The summer's flower is to the summer sweet,
Though to itself, it only live and die,
But if that flower with base infection meet,
The basest weed out-braves his dignity:
    For sweetest things turn sourest by their deeds,
    Lilies that fester, smell far worse then weeds.

A STATUE OF EROS

Who carved Love
      and placed him by
this fountain,
      thinking
he could control
      such fire
with water?

ZENODOTOS (*b.* 325 BC),
TRANS. PETER JAY

THE WOUNDED CUPID. SONG

Cupid as he lay among
Roses, by a Bee was stung.
Whereupon in anger flying
To his Mother, said thus crying;
Help! O help! your Boy's a dying.
And why, my pretty Lad, said she?
Then blubbering, replied he,
A winged Snake has bitten me,
Which Country people call a Bee.
At which she smil'd; then with her hairs
And kisses drying up his tears:
Alas! said she, my Wag! if this
Such a pernicious torment is:
Come, tell me then, how great's the smart
Of those, thou woundest with thy Dart!

ANACREON (6TH CENTURY BC),
TRANS. ROBERT HERRICK (1591–1674)

LOVE THOU ART HIGH

Love – thou art high –
I cannot climb thee –
But, were it Two –
Who knows but we –
Taking turns – at the Chimborazo –
Ducal – at last – stand up by thee –

Love – thou art deep –
I cannot cross thee –
But, were there Two
Instead of One –
Rower, and Yacht – some sovereign Summer –
Who knows – but we'd reach the Sun?

Love – thou art Veiled –
A few – behold thee –
Smile – and alter – and prattle – and die –
Bliss – were an Oddity – without thee –
Nicknamed by God –
Eternity –

LOVE IS THAT LATER THING

Love – is that later Thing than Death –
More previous – than Life –
Confirms it at its entrance – And
Usurps it – of itself –

Tastes Death – the first – to hand the sting
The Second – to its friend –
Disarms the little interval –
Deposits Him with God –

Then hovers – an inferior Guard –
Lest this Beloved Charge
Need – once in an Eternity –
A smaller than the Large –

TO HIS COY MISTRESS

Had we but world enough, and time,
This coyness, Lady, were no crime.
We would sit down and think which way
To walk and pass our long love's day.
Thou by the Indian Ganges' side
Shouldst rubies find: I by the tide
Of Humber would complain. I would
Love you ten years before the Flood,
And you should, if you please, refuse
Till the conversion of the Jews.
My vegetable love should grow
Vaster than empires, and more slow;
An hundred years should go to praise
Thine eyes and on thy forehead gaze;
Two hundred to adore each breast;
But thirty thousand to the rest;
An age at least to every part,
And the last age should show your heart;
For, Lady, you deserve this state,
Nor would I love at lower rate.

But at my back I always hear
Time's wingèd chariot hurrying near;
And yonder all before us lie
Deserts of vast eternity.

Thy beauty shall no more be found,
Nor, in thy marble vault, shall sound
My echoing song: then worms shall try
That long preserved virginity,
And your quaint honour turn to dust,
And into ashes all my lust:
The grave's a fine and private place,
But none, I think, do there embrace.

    Now therefore, while the youthful hue
Sits on thy skin like morning dew,
And while thy willing soul transpires
At every pore with instant fires,
Now let us sport us while we may,
And now, like amorous birds of prey,
Rather at once our time devour
Than languish in his slow-chapt power.
Let us roll all our strength and all
Our sweetness up into one ball,
And tear our pleasures with rough strife
Thorough the iron gates of life:
Thus, though we cannot make our sun
Stand still, yet we will make him run.

ANDREW MARVELL (1621–1678)   37

TO HIS MISTRESS GOING TO BED

Come, Madam, come, all rest my powers defy,
Until I labour, I in labour lie.
The foe oft-times having the foe in sight,
Is tir'd with standing though he never fight.
Off with that girdle, like heaven's Zone glistering,
But a far fairer world encompassing.
Unpin that spangled breastplate which you wear,
That th'eyes of busy fools may be stopped there.
Unlace yourself, for that harmonious chime,
Tells me from you, that now it is bed time.
Off with that happy busk, which I envy,
That still can be, and still can stand so nigh.
Your gown going off, such beauteous state reveals,
As when from flowery meads th'hill's shadow steals.
Off with that wiry Coronet and shew
The hairy Diadem which on you doth grow:
Now off with those shoes, and then safely tread
In this love's hallow'd temple, this soft bed.
In such white robes, heaven's Angels used to be
Received by men; Thou Angel bringst with thee
A heaven like Mahomet's Paradise; and though
Ill spirits walk in white, we easily know,
By this these Angels from an evil sprite,
Those set our hairs, but these our flesh upright.

Licence my roving hands, and let them go,
Before, behind, between, above, below.
O my America! my new-found-land,
My kingdom, safeliest when with one man mann'd,
My Mine of precious stones, My Empirie,
How blest am I in this discovering thee!
To enter in these bonds, is to be free;
Then where my hand is set, my seal shall be.
    Full nakedness! All joys are due to thee,
As souls unbodied, bodies uncloth'd must be,
To taste whole joys. Gems which you women use
Are like Atlanta's balls, cast in men's views,
That when a fool's eye lighteth on a Gem,
His earthly soul may covet theirs, not them.
Like pictures, or like books' gay coverings made
For lay-men, are all women thus array'd;
Themselves are mystic books, which only we
(Whom their imputed grace will dignify)
Must see reveal'd. Then since that I may know;
As liberally, as to a Midwife, shew
Thy self: cast all, yea, this white linen hence,
There is no penance due to innocence.
    To teach thee, I am naked first; why then
What needst thou have more covering than a man.

TO THE VIRGINS,
TO MAKE MUCH OF TIME

Gather ye rosebuds while ye may,
    Old Time is still a-flying:
And this same flower that smiles today
    Tomorrow will be dying.

The glorious lamp of heaven, the sun,
    The higher he's a-getting,
The sooner will his race be run,
    And nearer he's to setting.

That age is best which is the first,
    When youth and blood are warmer;
But being spent, the worse, and worst
    Times still succeed the former.

Then be not coy, but use your time,
    And while ye may, go marry:
For having lost but once your prime,
    You may for ever tarry.

THYRSIS AND AMARANTA (Fables, VIII, 13)

Let's bring some shepherds on for now, and rhyme
The talk of wolves and sheep some other time.

Thyrsis last Sunday was improving Amaranta's
      Young mind: 'I wish you knew
This illness that I have – you'd want to have it too –
    It pleases and enchants us –
There's nothing good, this side of heaven, to match it.
    Please let me help you catch it –
    Believe me, don't be scared – be bold.
Would I trick *you*? – for whom I'm proud to say
I have the kindest feelings any heart can hold.'

    She answered straight away:
'What is this illness called? It has a name, I guess?'
   'Amour.' 'A pretty word. Tell me some things
To know it by – the symptoms, more or less.'
   'You get such pains the ecstasy of kings
Is dull and boring in comparison
      With this condition.
   You quite forget yourself – you could
Be happy, solitary in a wood.
   You lean and look into a stream:

41

You don't see you, you only see this dream
Which recurs everywhere and endlessly.
Except for that, you have no eyes to see.
   There is a shepherd, where you're from,
     The sight or voice of whom,
   Even the name, can make you blush.
You think of him, your breath comes in a rush:
      You sigh; you don't know why;
       And yet you sigh,
Afraid you'll see him, though you long to see him.'

Here Amaranta gives a little scream:
'Oh that's the illness that you praise sky-high!
It isn't new to me: I think I know it.'
   Thyrsis, the shepherd poet,
Thinks now he's hit the target that he fancies –
When the girl adds, 'That shyness in a trance is
Exactly what I feel for Clidamantes.'

Poor fellow thought he'd die of shame and chagrin.
   He's not alone, though. Lots imagine
They're acting for themselves, and then discover
They're done the bargaining for some other lover.

42   JEAN DE LA FONTAINE (1621–1695),
    TRANS. ALISTAIR ELLIOT

COME QUICKLY

Come quickly – as soon as
these blossoms open,
they fall.
This world exists
as a sheen of dew on flowers.

IZUMI SHIKIBU (?974–?1034),   43
TRANS. JANE HIRSHFIELD AND MARIKO ARATANI

INVITATION TO JUNO

Lucretius could not credit centaurs;
Such bicycle he deemed asynchronous.
'Man superannuates the horse;
Horse pulses will not gear with ours.'

Johnson could see no bicycle would go;
'You bear yourself, and the machine as well.'
Gennets for germans sprang not from Othello,
And Ixion rides upon a single wheel.

Courage. Weren't strips of heart culture seen
Of late mating two periodicities?
Could not Professor Charles Darwin
Graft annual upon perennial trees?

GO, LOVELY ROSE

Go, lovely Rose –
    Tell her that wastes her time and me,
    That now she knows,
When I resemble her to thee,
How sweet and fair she seems to be.

    Tell her that's young,
And shuns to have her graces spied,
    That hadst thou sprung
In deserts where no men abide,
Thou must have uncommended died.

    Small is the worth
Of beauty from the light retired:
    Bid her come forth,
Suffer herself to be desired,
And not blush so to be admired.

    Then die – that she
The common fate of all things rare
    May read in thee;
How small a part of time they share
That are so wondrous sweet and fair!

CORINNA IN VENDOME

Darling, each morning a blooded rose
Lures the sunlight in, and shows
Her soft, moist and secret part.
See now, before you go to bed,
Her skirts replaced, her deeper red –
A colour much like yours, dear heart.

Alas, her petals will blow away,
Her beauties in a single day
Vanish like ashes on the wind.
O savage Time! that what we prize
Should flutter down before our eyes –
Who also, late or soon, descend.

Then scatter, darling, your caresses
While you may, and wear green dresses;
Gather roses, gather me –
Tomorrow, aching for your charms,
Death shall take you in his arms
And shatter your virginity.

PIERRE DE RONSARD (1524–1585),
TRANS. ALISTAIR ELLIOT

LOVE AND POETRY

LOVING IN TRUTH

Loving in truth, and fain in verse my love to show,
That she, dear she, might take some pleasure of
    my pain:
Pleasure might cause her read, reading might make
    her know,
Knowledge might pity win, and pity grace obtain,
  I sought fit words to paint the blackest face of woe,
Studying inventions fine, her wits to entertain:
Oft turning others' leaves to see if thence would flow
Some fresh and fruitful showers upon my sun-burn'd
    brain.
  But words came halting forth, wanting Invention's
    stay,
Invention, Nature's child, fled step-dame Study's blows,
And others' feet still seem'd but strangers in my way.
Thus great with child to speak, and helpless in my
    throes,
  Biting my trewand pen, beating myself for spite,
  Fool, said my Muse to me, look in thy heart and
    write.

MY DOWNFALL

My downfall: those pink articulate lips
Divinely flavoured portals to a mouth
Where soul dissolves ... eyes darting
Beneath black brows, snares for the heart,
And the milk-white breasts, well shaped,
The twin rosebuds, fair beyond other flowers.

To itemize thus – is this to cast dogs a bone?
The poet's pen – secret as reeds of Midas?

HER WORDS

A young mouth laughs at a gift.
She croons, like a cat to its claws;
Cries, 'I'm old enough to live
And delight in a lover's praise,
Yet keep to myself my own mind;
I dance to the right, to the left;
My luck raises the wind.'

'Write all my whispers down,'
She cries to her true love.
'I believe, I believe, in the moon! —
What weather of heaven is this?'

'The storm, the storm of a kiss.'

TONIGHT I CAN WRITE

Tonight I can write the saddest lines.

Write, for example, 'The night is shattered
and the blue stars shiver in the distance.'

The night wind revolves in the sky and sings.

Tonight I can write the saddest lines.
I loved her, and sometimes she loved me too.

Through nights like this one I held her in my arms.
I kissed her again and again under the endless sky.

She loved me, sometimes I loved her too.
How could one not have loved her great still eyes.

Tonight I can write the saddest lines.
To think that I do not have her. To feel that I have
    lost her.

To hear the immense night, still more immense
    without her.
And the verse falls to the soul like dew to the pasture.

What does it matter that my love could not keep her.
The night is shattered and she is not with me.

This is all. In the distance someone is singing. In the
    distance.
My soul is not satisfied that it has lost her.

My sight searches for her as though to go to her.
My heart looks for her, and she is not with me.

The same night whitening the same trees.
We, of that time, are no longer the same.

I no longer love her, that's certain, but how I loved her.
My voice tried to find the wind to touch her hearing.

Another's. She will be another's. Like my kisses before.
Her voice, her bright body. Her infinite eyes.

I no longer love her, that's certain, but maybe I love her.
Love is so short, forgetting is so long.

Because through nights like this one I held her in
      my arms
my soul is not satisfied that it has lost her.

Though this be the last pain that she makes me suffer
and these the last verses that I write for her.

I KNOW THAT ALL BENEATH
THE MOON DECAYS

I know that all beneath the moon decays,
And what by mortals in this world is brought,
In Time's great periods shall return to nought;
That fairest states have fatal nights and days;
I know how all the Muse's heavenly lays,
With toil of spright which are so dearly bought,
As idle sounds of few or none are sought,
And that nought lighter is than airy praise.
I know frail beauty like the purple flower,
To which one morn oft birth and death affords;
That love a jarring is of minds' accords,
Where sense and will invassal reason's power:
Know what I list, this all can not me move,
But that, O me! I both must write and love.

DARLING, IT'S FRIGHTENING

Darling, it's frightening! When a poet loves
he might be an unshriven god enraptured.
And chaos creeps again up to the light,
as in the far off ages of the fossils.

His eyes weep tons of billows and he's swathed
in cloud, so that you'd take him for a mammoth.
He's out of date. He knows it's no more use.
His days are over now and he's illiterate.

He sees the way his neighbours hold their weddings,
how they get roaring drunk and sleep it off,
how they call common roe – that pickled frogspawn, –
once she's been married off, the best pressed caviare.

And how they manage to squeeze in a snuff-box
life that is like a pearly dream by Watteau.
They take revenge on him; perhaps it's only
because, while they are twisting and contorting,

while sniggering bourgeois comfort lies and flatters
and they rub shoulders with the drones and crawl,
he's raised a girl like you from earth and used her,
like a Bacchante from her amphora.

And thawing of the Andes melts in kisses
and morning's on the steppe, beneath the dominion
of stars that fall in dust, as night goes stumbling
with bleat growing ever paler, through the village.

And round the straw bed's fevered pain breathe all
the exhalations of the ancient pit
and all the vestry's gloomy vegetation.
And chaos splashes up out of the jungle.

PRAISING THE
LOVED ONE

TO THE LADY RADEGUND, WITH VIOLETS

If 'twere the time of lilies,
    Or of the crimson rose,
I'd pluck them in the fields for you,
    Or my poor garden close:
Small gift for you so rare.

But I can find no lilies,
    Green herbs are all I bring.
Yet love makes vetches roses,
    And in their shadowing
Hide violets as fair.

For royal is their purple,
    And fragrant is their breath,
And to one sweet and royal,
    Their fragrance witnesseth
Beauty abiding there.

VENANTIUS FORTUNATUS (*c.* 540–*c.* 600),   61
TRANS. HELEN WADDELL (1889–1965)

I WILL LEAVE YOUR WHITE HOUSE

I will leave your white house and tranquil garden.
Let life be empty and bright.
You, and only you, I shall glorify in my poems,
As a woman has never been able to do.
And you remember the beloved
For whose eyes you created this paradise,
But I deal in rare commodities –
I sell your love and tenderness.

62   ANNA AKHMATOVA (1889–1966),
     TRANS. JUDITH HEMSCHEMEYER

A SONG OF CHANG CHING-YÜAN PICKING LOTUS FLOWERS

Essence of orchids in her tumbled hair, a goddess of
    spring,
She takes the swallow hairpin from her nape, loosens
    coiled tresses.
Under the willows by west gate, near the bridge at dusk,
Moated waters past doorways, dabbled, riffled flow.
A prince of rare talents, visitor to the imperial court,
Shell fittings on his saddle all a-jangle, crosses the
    spring lane.

Dancing effortlessly on an open palm, her sheer skirt,
Tailored shagreen dress, best the colors of spring.
Like wafting smoke embracing the moon, waist one
    measure round,
Scent of musk and dragon marrow, how lovely,
    graceful is she!

Clouds like autumn curtains brush the water –
    fragments of bright movement;
Dew-laden, flowers in profusion, their fragrance
    unfading.
Mandarin ducks go to and fro on the brimming pond,
'Midst duckweeds green like tassels, and short lotus
    stems.

One evening the west wind comes bringing showers,
Scaring, stripping bare the flowers, a melancholy pale
    red.
Boat prows sever lotus stems, but strands unseen hold
    fast,
For lotus roots, lotus seeds, preserve a mutual bond.
His heart is like the moon, a moon not yet on the wane,
Clear, bright and full of mid-month days.

64   WÊN T'ING-YÜN (?813–870),
    TRANS. WILLIAM R. SCHULTZ

YOU'RE HERE

You're here. We breathe the selfsame air.
Your presence here is like the city,
like quiet Kiev wrapped in sultry
sunbeams there outside the window.

It hasn't slept its sleep out yet,
but struggles in its dreams, unconquered.
It tears the bricks from off its neck
like a sweaty Shantung collar.

In it, perspiring in their leaves
from obstacles they've just got over,
the poplars gather in a crowd
wearily on the conquered pavement.

You make me think the Dnieper there,
in its green skin of creeks and ditches,
the centre-of-the-earth's complaint book
for us to write our daily notes in.

Your presence here is like a call
to sit down hastily at midday,
to read it through from A to Z
and then to write your nearness in it.

BORIS PASTERNAK (1890–1960),
TRANS. J. M. COWEN

65

ONE GIRL

I

Like the sweet apple which reddens upon
    the topmost bough,
Atop on the topmost twig, – which the
    pluckers forgot, somehow, –
Forgot it not, nay; but got it not, for none
    could get it till now.

II

Like the wild hyacinth flower which on the
    hills is found,
Which the passing feet of the shepherds
    for ever tear and wound,
Until the purple blossom is trodden in the
    ground.

SAPPHO (7TH CENTURY BC),
TRANS. DANTE GABRIEL ROSSETTI (1828–1882)

MY MISTRESS' EYES ARE
NOTHING LIKE THE SUN

My mistress' eyes are nothing like the sun;
Coral is far more red than her lips' red:
If snow be white, why then her breasts are dun;
If hairs be wires, black wires grow on her head.
I have seen roses damaskt, red and white,
But no such roses see I in her cheeks;
And in some perfumes is there more delight
Than in the breath that from my mistress reeks.
I love to hear her speak, yet well I know
That music hath a far more pleasing sound;
I grant I never saw a goddess go;
My mistress, when she walks, treads on the ground.
　　And yet, by heaven, I think my love as rare
　　As any she belied with false compare.

NOT MARBLE, NOR
THE GILDED MONUMENTS

Not marble, nor the gilded monuments
Of princes, shall outlive this powerful rhyme;
But you shall shine more bright in these contents
Than unswept stone, besmear'd with sluttish time.
When wasteful war shall statues overturn,
And broils root out the work of masonry,
Nor Mars his sword nor war's quick fire shall burn
The living record of your memory.
'Gainst death and all-oblivious enmity
Shall you pace forth; your praise shall still find room
Even in the eyes of all posterity
That wear this world out to the ending doom.
   So, till the judgement that yourself arise,
    You live in this, and dwell in lovers' eyes.

LOVE SONG

Sweep the house clean,
hang fresh curtains
in the windows
put on a new dress
and come with me!
The elm is scattering
its little loaves
of sweet smells
from a white sky!
Who shall hear of us
in the time to come?
Let him say there was
a burst of fragrance
from black branches.

DEVOTION IS A HEAVY CROSS

Devotion is a heavy cross,
but you are lovely and direct;
the mystery of your attractions
is powerful as the key to life.

Scuffling of dreams is heard in spring,
rustle of news and truths. And your
family sprang from such beginnings.
Your mind's impartial as the air.

Lightly to waken, see again,
shake from the heart its wordy litter
and live in future days unchoked,
surely all that needs no great cunning.

BORIS PASTERNAK (1890–1960),
TRANS. J. M. COWEN

WILLOW

Awakening spring: how many leaves!
Rustling dawn: how many branches!
Does she know the pangs of love?
Never a time she wouldn't dance.

Pussy willows aflutter – hide white butterfly,
Tendrils hanging limp – bare yellow oriole.
All-conquering beauty, perfect through and through:
Who would enjoy just the brows of her eyes?

LI SHANG-YIN (?813–858),   71
TRANS. EUGENE EOYANG AND IRVING Y. LO

THE RIVAL

If the moon smiled, she would resemble you.
You leave the same impression
Of something beautiful, but annihilating.
Both of you are great light borrowers.
Her O-mouth grieves at the world; yours is unaffected,

And your first gift is making stone out of everything.
I wake to a mausoleum; you are here,
Ticking your fingers on the marble table, looking for
        cigarettes,
Spiteful as a woman, but not so nervous,
And dying to say something unanswerable.

The moon, too, abases her subjects,
But in the daytime she is ridiculous.
Your dissatisfactions, on the other hand,
Arrive through the mailslot with loving regularity,
White and blank, expansive as carbon monoxide.

No day is safe from news of you,
Walking about in Africa maybe, but thinking of me.

I WISHED, ALL THE MILD DAYS OF
MIDDLE MARCH

I wished, all the mild days of middle March
This special year, your blond good-nature might
(Lady) admit – kicking abruptly tight
With will and affection down your breast like starch –
Me to your story, in Spring, and stretch, and arch.
But who not flanks the wells of uncanny light
Sudden in bright sand towering? A bone sunned white.
Considering travellers bypass these and parch.

This came to less yes than an ice cream cone
Let stand ... though still my sense of it is brisk:
Blond silky cream, sweet cold, aches: a door shut.
Errors of order! Luck lies with the bone,
Who rushed (and rests) to meet your small mouth, risk
Your teeth irregular and passionate.

TO HELEN

Helen, thy beauty is to me
    Like those Nicean barks of yore,
That gently, o'er a perfumed sea,
    The weary, wayworn wanderer bore
    To his own native shore.

On desperate seas long wont to roam,
    Thy hyacinth hair, thy classic face,
Thy Naiad airs have brought me home
    To the glory that was Greece,
    To the grandeur that was Rome.

Lo! in yon brilliant window niche,
    How statue-like I see thee stand,
    The agate lamp within thy hand!
Ah, Psyche, from the regions which
    Are Holy Land!

HELEN

I am the blue! I come from the lower world
to hear the serene erosion of the surf;
once more I see the galleys bleed with dawn,
and shark with muffled rowlocks into Troy.
My solitary hands recall the kings;
I used to run my fingers through their beards;
I wept. They sang about their shady wars,
the great gulfs boiling sternward from their keels.
I hear the military trumpets, all that brass,
blasting commands to the frantic oars;
the rowers' metronome enchains the sea,
and high on beaked and dragon prows, the gods –
their fixed, archaic smiles stung by the salt –
reach out their carved, indulgent arms to me!

PAUL VALÉRY (1871–1945),
TRANS. ROBERT LOWELL (1917–1977)

SONNET FOR HELEN

Since she's all winter, with a heart of snow
Plated in ice and armed with icicles,
And loves me only for these canticles,
I'm mad not to undo my bonds and go.
    What use to me are her great name and race? –
Beautiful prisons, well-bred slavery.
– Mistress, my hair's not gone so grey on me
Another heart won't gladly take your place.

Love is a child and does not hide the truth:
You may be proud, and rich in beauty too,
But not enough to scorn a heart that's true;
    I can't re-enter April and my youth.
Grey though my head is now, love me today,
And I shall love you when your own is grey.

76   PIERRE DE RONSARD (1524–1585),
       TRANS. ALISTAIR ELLIOT

I KNEW A WOMAN

I knew a woman, lovely in her bones,
When small birds sighed, she would sigh back at them;
Ah, when she moved, she moved more ways than one:
The shapes a bright container can contain!
Of her choice virtues only gods should speak,
Or English poets who grew up on Greek
(I'd have them sing in chorus, cheek to cheek).

How well her wishes went! She stroked my chin,
She taught me Turn, and Counter-turn, and Stand;
She taught me Touch, that undulant white skin;
I nibbled meekly from her proffered hand;
She was the sickle; I, poor I, the rake,
Coming behind her for her pretty sake
(But what prodigious mowing we did make).

Love likes a gander, and adores a goose:
Her full lips pursed, the errant note to seize;
She played it quick, she played it light and loose;
My eyes, they dazzled at her flowing knees;
Her several parts could keep a pure repose,
Or one hip quiver with a mobile nose
(She moved in circles, and those circles moved).

Let seed be grass, and grass turn into hay:
I'm martyr to a motion not my own;
What's freedom for? To know eternity.
I swear she cast a shadow white as stone.
But who would count eternity in days?
These old bones live to learn her wanton ways:
(I measure time by how a body sways).

FISH IN THE UNRUFFLED LAKES

Fish in the unruffled lakes
The swarming colours wear,
Swans in the winter air
A white perfection have,
And the great lion walks
Through his innocent grove;
Lion, fish, and swan
Act, and are gone
Upon Time's toppling wave.

We till shadowed days are done,
We must weep and sing
Duty's conscious wrong,
The Devil in the clock,
The Goodness carefully worn
For atonement or for luck;
We must lose our loves,
On each beast and bird that moves
Turn an envious look.

Sighs for folly said and done
Twist our narrow days;
But I must bless, I must praise
That you, my swan, who have
All gifts that to the swan
Impulsive Nature gave,
The majesty and pride,
Last night should add
Your voluntary love.

IN MY SKY AT TWILIGHT

*This poem is a paraphrase of the 30th poem
in Rabindranath Tagore's* The Gardener.

In my sky at twilight you are like a cloud
and your form and colour are the way I love them.
You are mine, mine, woman with sweet lips
and in your life my infinite dreams live.

The lamp of my soul dyes your feet,
the sour wine is sweeter on your lips,
oh reaper of my evening song,
how solitary dreams believe you to be mine!

You are mine, mine, I go shouting it to the afternoon's
wind, and the wind hauls on my widowed voice.
Huntress of the depths of my eyes, your plunder
stills your nocturnal regard as though it were water.

You are taken in the net of my music, my love,
and my nets of music are wide as the sky.
My soul is born on the shore of your eyes of mourning.
In your eyes of mourning the land of dreams begins.

PABLO NERUDA (1904–1973),   81
TRANS. W. S. MERWIN

NEVER AGAIN WOULD BIRDS' SONG
BE THE SAME

He would declare and could himself believe
That the birds there in all the garden round
From having heard the daylong voice of Eve
Had added to their own an oversound,
Her tone of meaning but without the words.
Admittedly an eloquence so soft
Could only have had an influence on birds
When call or laughter carried it aloft.
Be that as may be, she was in their song.
Moreover her voice upon their voices crossed
Had now persisted in the woods so long
That probably it never would be lost.
Never again would birds' song be the same.
And to do that to birds was why she came.

THE LOVE A LIFE CAN SHOW

The Love a Life can show Below
Is but a filament, I know,
Of that diviner thing
That faints upon the face of Noon –
And smites the Tinder in the Sun –
And hinders Gabriel's Wing –

'Tis this – in Music – hints and sways –
And far abroad on Summer days –
Distils uncertain pain –
'Tis this enamors in the East –
And tints the Transit in the West
With harrowing Iodine –

'Tis this – invites – appalls – endows –
Flits – glimmers – proves – dissolves –
Returns – suggests – convicts – enchants –
Then – flings in Paradise –

HER FACE

Her face	Her tongue	Her wit
so fair	so sweet	so sharp
first bent	then drew	then hit
mine eye	mine ear	my heart

Mine eye	Mine ear	My heart
to like	to learn	to love
her face	her tongue	her wit
doth lead	doth teach	doth move

Her face	Her tongue	Her wit
with beams	with sound	with art
doth blind	doth charm	doth knit
mine eye	mine ear	my heart

Mine eye	Mine ear	My heart
with life	with hope	with skill
her face	her tongue	her wit
doth feed	doth feast	doth fill

O face	O tongue	O wit
with frowns	with checks	with smart
wrong not	vex not	wound not
mine eye	mine ear	my heart

This eye	This ear	This heart
shall joy	shall yield	shall swear
her face	her tongue	her wit
to serve	to trust	to fear.

From THE SONG OF SOLOMON

CHAPTER 2

I am the rose of Sharon, and the lily of the valleys.

As the lily among thorns, so is my love among the daughters.

As the apple tree among the trees of the wood, so is my beloved among the sons. I sat down under his shadow with great delight, and his fruit was sweet to my taste.

He brought me to the banqueting house, and his banner over me was love.

Stay me with flagons, comfort me with apples: for I am sick of love.

His left hand is under my head, and his right hand doth embrace me.

I charge you, O ye daughters of Jerusalem, by the roes, and by the hinds of the field, that ye stir not up, nor awake my love, till he please.

The voice of my beloved! behold, he cometh leaping upon the mountains, skipping upon the hills.

My beloved is like a roe or a young hart: behold, he standeth behind our wall, he looketh forth at the windows, showing himself through the lattice.

My beloved spake, and said unto me, Rise up, my love, my fair one, and come away.

For, lo, the winter is past, the rain is over and gone;

The flowers appear on the earth; the time of the singing of birds is come, and the voice of the turtle is heard in our land:

The fig tree putteth forth her green figs, and the vines with the tender grape give a good smell. Arise, my love, my fair one, and come away.

O my dove, that art in the clefts of the rock, in the secret places of the stairs, let me see thy countenance, let me hear thy voice; for sweet is thy voice, and thy countenance is comely.

Take us the foxes, the little foxes, that spoil the vines; for our vines have tender grapes.

My beloved is mine, and I am his: he feedeth among the lilies.

Until the day break, and the shadows flee away, turn, my beloved, and be thou like a roe or a young hart upon the mountains of Bether.

A SONG

Ask me no more where Jove bestows,
When June is past, the fading rose;
For in your beauty's orient deep
These flowers, as in their causes, sleep.

Ask me no more whither do stray
The golden atoms of the day;
For in pure love heaven did prepare
Those powders to enrich your hair.

Ask me no more whither doth haste
The nightingale, when May is past;
For in your sweet dividing throat
She winters, and keeps warm her note.

Ask me no more where those stars 'light,
That downwards fall in dead of night;
For in your eyes they sit, and there
Fixed become, as in their sphere.

Ask me no more if east or west
The phœnix builds her spicy nest;
For unto you at last she flies,
And in your fragrant bosom dies.

88   THOMAS CAREW (1594/5–1640)

THE SUN RISING

Busy old fool, unruly Sun,
    Why dost thou thus,
Through windows, and through curtains call on us?
Must to thy motions lovers' seasons run?
    Saucy pedantic wretch, go chide
    Late school-boys, and sour 'prentices,
  Go tell court-huntsmen that the King will ride,
  Call country ants to harvest offices;
Love, all alike, no season knows, nor clime,
Nor hours, days, months, which are the rags of time.

    Thy beams, so reverend, and strong
    Why shouldst thou think?
I could eclipse and cloud them with a wink,
But that I would not lose her sight so long:
    If her eyes have not blinded thine,
    Look, and tomorrow late, tell me,
  Whether both the Indias of spice and mine
  Be where thou left'st them, or lie here with me.
Ask for those kings whom thou saw'st yesterday,
And thou shalt hear, 'All here in one bed lay.'

She is all States, and all Princes, I;
    Nothing else is.
Princes do but play us; compar'd to this,
All honour's mimic; all wealth alchemy.
    Thou Sun art half as happy as we,
      In that the world's contracted thus;
    Thine age asks ease, and since thy duties be
    To warm the world, that's done in warming us.
Shine here to us, and thou art every where;
This bed thy centre is, these walls, thy sphere.

SHE WALKS IN BEAUTY

She walks in beauty, like the night
    Of cloudless climes and starry skies;
And all that's best of dark and bright
    Meet in her aspect and her eyes:
Thus mellowed to that tender light
    Which heaven to gaudy day denies.

One shade the more, one ray the less,
    Had half impaired the nameless grace
Which waves in every raven tress,
    Or softly lightens o'er her face;
Where thoughts serenely sweet express
    How pure, how dear their dwelling place.

And on that cheek, and o'er that brow,
    So soft, so calm, yet eloquent,
The smiles that win, the tints that glow,
    But tell of days in goodness spent,
A mind at peace with all below,
    A heart whose love is innocent!

LORD BYRON (1788–1824)   91

THE LORD IS NOT MERCIFUL

The Lord is not merciful to reapers and gardeners.
A ringing rain slants down
And wide cloaks are going to color
The sky reflected in the water.

There's an underwater kingdom of meadows
    and cornfields,
And undulating streams sing out, sing out,
On the swelling branches plums are bursting
And the flattened grasses rot.

And through the dense scrim of water
I see your dear face,
The hushed park, the Chinese Pavilion
And the circular porch of the house.

ANNA AKHMATOVA (1889–1966),
TRANS. JUDITH HEMSCHEMEYER

THE PORTRAIT

She speaks always in her own voice
Even to strangers; but those other women
Exercise their borrowed, or false, voices
Even on sons and daughters.

She can walk invisibly at noon
Along the high road; but those other women
Gleam phosphorescent – broad hips and gross fingers –
Down every lampless alley.

She is wild and innocent, pledged to love
Through all disaster; but those other women
Decry her for a witch or a common drab
And glare back when she greets them.

Here is her portrait, gazing sidelong at me,
The hair in disarray, the young eyes pleading:
'And you, love? As unlike those other men
As I those other women?'

ROBERT GRAVES (1895–1985)   93

THE EEL

I

The eel, the North Sea siren,
who leaves dead-pan Icelandic gods
and the Baltic for our Mediterranean,
our estuaries, our rivers –
who lances through their profound places,
and flinty portages, from branch to branch,
twig to twig, thinning down now,
ever snaking inward, worming
for the granite's heartland, threading
delicate capillaries of slime –
and in the Romagna one morning
the blaze of the chestnut blossoms
ignites its smudge in the dead water
pooled from chisellings
of the Apennines . . .
the eel, a whipstock, a Roman candle,
love's arrow on earth, which only
reaches the paradise of fecundity
through our gullies and fiery, charred streams;
a green spirit, potent only
where desolation and arson burn;
a spark that says everything
begins where everything is clinker;
this buried rainbow, this iris, twin sister

of the one you set in your eye's target centre
to shine on the sons of men,
on us, up to our gills in your life-giving mud –
can you call her *Sister*?

II

If they called you a fox,
it will be for your monstrous hurtle,
your sprint that parts and unites,
that kicks up and freshens the gravel,
(your black lace balcony, overlooking
the home for deformed children, a meadow,
and a tree, where my carved name quivers,
happy, humble, defeated) –
or perhaps only for the phosphorescent wake
of your almond eyes,
for the craft of your alert panic,
for the annihilation of dishevelled feathers
in your child's hand's python hug;
if they have likened you to the blond lioness,
to the avaricious demon of the undergrowth
(and why not to the filthy fish
that electrocutes, the torpedo fish?)
it is perhaps because the blind
have not seen the wings
on your delectable shoulder-blades,
because the blind haven't shot for

your forehead's luminous target,
the furrow I pricked there in blood,
cross, chrism, incantation, – and
prayer – damnation, salvation;
if they can only think of you
as a weasel or a woman,
with whom can I share my discovery,
where bury the gold I carry,
the red-hot, pot-bellied furnace raging
inside me, when, leaving me,
you turn up stairs?

EUGENIO MONTALE (1896–1981),
TRANS. ROBERT LOWELL (1917–1977)

THE PALANQUIN

In a thin cloud of cool and glowing muslin
  You would come down
The hill-slopes in a palanquin of rattan
  On Sunday mornings into town.

The church bell would be tapping out its warning,
  The sea wind stroking fields of cane;
Like golden hail, the crackling fire of sunlight
  Beat on the tassels of the plain.

With bracelets on both wrists, and rings on ankles,
  And yellow kerchiefs in their plaits,
Your two Telingas, constant followers, carried
  Your bed with its Manila mats.

Flickering lean and sinewy hams, unhindered
  By their white tunics, with a song
They'd go, with hands on hips, bamboo on shoulders,
  To the Lagoon and then along –

Along the causeway by the low verandas
  Where the old creoles sat to smoke,
They'd quicken, hearing Malagasy music,
  Past groups of black men howling at a joke.

In the light air the smell of tamarinds floated;
   And on the backlit swell, always,
Far out, the endless skeins of seabirds diving
   Into the deep-sea haze.

Sometimes your foot, escaping from its slipper,
   Hung, pink, over the hammock's edges,
In the thick shade of black-wood trees and bushes
   With fruit less purple than your mouth, the litchis;

Sometimes a butterfly with flowering wings,
   Patterned bright red and blue,
Would light a moment on the delicate skin,
   Transferring colours onto you,

While one half-saw your curls against the pillow
   Shine golden through the curtains of batiste,
And under half-closed eyelids, as if drowsy,
   Your lovely eyes' dark amethyst.

So you would come, those sweet and peaceful
      mornings,
   Rocked by your Hindoos' rhythmic pace,
Out of the mountains for Communion, rosy
   With youth and full of native grace.

O charm of my first daydreams, now you lie
    With couch-grass overhead,
In barren sands, by groaning northern seas,
    At rest among my dearest dead.

LECONTE DE LISLE (1818–1894),
TRANS. ALISTAIR ELLIOT

PLEASURES
AND PAINS

WILD VINES

Beneath a willow entwined with ivy,
we look for shelter from the bad weather;
one raincoat covers both our shoulders –
my fingers rustle like the wild vine around
    your breasts.

I am wrong. The rain's stopped.
Not ivy, but the hair of Dionysus
hangs from these willows. What am I to do?
Throw the raincoat under us!

BORIS PASTERNAK (1890–1960), 103
TRANS. ROBERT LOWELL (1917–1977)

TO VENUS

Having after long desire
Won from my sweet enemy
Some advance on that delight
Her cruelty refuses me,

Venus, here I offer you
Pink and rose and violet,
Flowers whose little scarlet buds
Look so like her lips, still shut,

Lips that I have kissed three times,
Walking softly to her door
In the shadow of this bush –
And I couldn't kiss her more:

For I thought her mother hid
Listening to us somewhere near,
Watching everything we did –
I am trembling still with fear.

Now I give you only flowers;
But if you turn her sympathies,
And make her kindly to my tears
As she's lovely in my eyes,

Then I'll dedicate to you
By the Loire a myrtle tree,
And in your honour cut the bark
With these lines of poetry:

Thenot consecrated here
To Venus, on these river banks,
This myrtle; also all these flocks,
And himself, in grateful thanks.

CONJUNCTION

What happens afterwards, none need enquire:
They are poised there in conjunction, beyond time,
At an oak-tree top level with Paradise:
Its leafy tester unshaken where they stand
Palm to palm, mouth to mouth, beyond desire,
Perpetuating lark song, perfume, colour,
And the tremulous gasp of watchful winds,

Past all unbelief, we know them held
By peace and light and irrefragable love –
Twin paragons, our final selves, resistant
To the dull pull of earth dappled with shade:
Myself the forester, never known to abandon
His vigilant coursing of the greenwood's floor,
And you, dryad of dryads, never before
Yielding her whole heart to the enemy, man.

PHYLLIS AND CORYDON

Phyllis Corydon clutched to him
her head at rest beneath his chin.
He said, 'If I don't love you more
than ever maid was loved before
I shall (if this the years not prove)
in Afric or the Indian grove
some green-eyed lion serve for food.'
      Amor, to show that he was pleased,
      approvingly (in silence) sneezed.
Then Phyllis slightly raised her head
(her lips were full & wet & red)
to kiss the sweet eyes full of her:
'Corydon mine, with me prefer
always to serve unique Amor:
my softer flesh the fire licks
more greedily and deeper sticks.'
      Amor, to show that he was pleased,
      approvingly (in silence) sneezed.

So loving & loved so, they rove
between twin auspices of Love.
Corydon sets in his eye-lust
Phyllis before all other dust;
Phyllis on Corydon expends
her nubile toys, Love's dividends.
Could Venus yield more love-delight
than here she grants in Love's requite?

DRUNK AS DRUNK

Drunk as drunk on turpentine
From your open kisses,
Your wet body wedged
Between my wet body and the strake
Of our boat that is made out of flowers,
Feasted, we guide it – our fingers
Like tallows adorned with yellow metal –
Over the sky's hot rim,
The day's last breath in our sails.

Pinned by the sun between solstice
And equinox, drowsy and tangled together
We drifted for months and woke
With the bitter taste of land on our lips,
Eyelids all sticky, and we longed for lime
And the sound of a rope
Lowering a bucket down its well. Then,
We came by night to the Fortunate Isles,
And lay like fish
Under the net of our kisses.

PABLO NERUDA (1904–1973),   109
TRANS. W. S. MERWIN

CAME TO ME

Came to me –
     Who?
She.
     When?
In the dawn, afraid.

     What of?
Anger.
     Whose?
Her father's.
     Confide!

I kissed her twice.
     Where?
On her moist mouth.
     Mouth?

No.
     What, then?
Cornelian.
     How was it?
Sweet.

110   RŪDAKĪ (*d.* 954 AD),
      TRANS. BASIL BUNTING (1900–1985)

THE THIEVES

Lovers in the act dispense
With such meum-tuum sense
As might warningly reveal
What they must not pick or steal,
And their nostrum is to say:
'I and you are both away.'

After, when they disentwine
You from me and yours from mine,
Neither can be certain who
Was that I whose mine was you.
To the act again they go
More completely not to know.

Theft is theft and raid is raid
Though reciprocally made.
Lovers, the conclusion is
Doubled sighs and jealousies
In a single heart that grieves
For lost honour among thieves.

IN FORMER DAYS

In former days we'd both agree
That you were me, and I was you.
What has now happened to us two,
That you are you, and I am me?

BHARTṚHARI (5TH CENTURY)
TRANS. JOHN BROUGH

THE JEWELS

My well-beloved was stripped. Knowing my whim,
She wore her tinkling gems, but naught besides:
And showed such pride as, while her luck betides,
A sultan's favoured slave may show to him.

When it lets off its lively, crackling sound,
This blazing blend of metal crossed with stone,
Gives me an ectasy I've only known
Where league of sound and lustre can be found.

She let herself be loved: then, drowsy-eyed,
Smiled down from her high couch in languid ease.
My love was deep and gentle as the seas
And rose to her as to a cliff the tide.

My own approval of each dreamy pose,
Like a tamed tiger, cunningly she sighted:
And candour, with lubricity united,
Gave piquancy to every one she chose.

Her limbs and hips, burnished with changing lustres,
Before my eyes clairvoyant and serene,
Swanned themselves, undulating in their sheen;
Her breasts and belly, of my vine the clusters.

Like evil angels rose, my fancy twitting,
To kill the peace which over me she'd thrown,
And to disturb her from the crystal throne
Where, calm and solitary, she was sitting.

So swerved her pelvis that, in one design,
Antiope's white rump it seemed to graft
To a boy's torso, merging fore and aft.
The talc on her brown tan seemed half-divine.

The lamp resigned its dying flame. Within,
The hearth alone lit up the darkened air,
And every time it sighed a crimson flare
It drowned in blood that amber-coloured skin.

114 CHARLES BAUDELAIRE (1821–1867),
     TRANS. ROY CAMPBELL (1901–1957)

IN THE ORCHARD

Leave go my hands, let me catch breath and see;
Let the dew-fall drench either side of me;
   Clear apple-leaves are soft upon that moon
Seen sidelong like a blossom in the tree;
     And God, ah God, that day should be so soon.

The grass is thick and cool, it lets us lie.
Kissed upon either cheek and either eye,
   I turn to thee as some green afternoon
Turns toward sunset, and is loth to die;
     Ah God, ah God, that day should be so soon.

Lie closer, lean your face upon my side,
Feel where the dew fell that has hardly dried,
   Hear how the blood beats that went nigh to swoon;
The pleasure lives there when the sense has died,
     Ah God, ah God, that day should be so soon.

O my fair lord, I charge you leave me this:
It is not sweeter than a foolish kiss?
   Nay take it then, my flower, my first in June,
My rose, so like a tender mouth it is:
     Ah God, ah God, that day should be so soon.

Love, till dawn sunder night from day with fire
Dividing my delight and my desire,
    The crescent life and love the plenilune,
Love me though dusk begin and dark retire;
    Ah God, ah God, that day should be so soon.

Ah, my heart fails, my blood draws back; I know,
When life runs over, life is near to go;
    And with the slain of love love's ways are strewn,
And with their blood, if love will have it so;
    Ah God, ah God, that day should be so soon.

Ah, do thy will now; slay me if thou wilt;
There is no building now the walls are built,
    No quarrying now the corner-stone is hewn,
No drinking now the vine's whole blood is spilt;
    Ah God, ah God, that day should be so soon.

Nay, slay me now; nay, for I will be slain;
Pluck thy red pleasure from the teeth of pain,
    Break down thy vine ere yet grape-gatherers prune,
Slay me ere day can slay desire again;
    Ah God, ah God, that day should be so soon.

Yea, with thy sweet lips, with thy sweet sword; yea
Take life and all, for I will die, I say;
    Love, I gave love, is life a better boon?
For sweet night's sake I will not live till day;
    Ah God, ah God, that day should be so soon.

Nay, I will sleep then only; nay, but go.
Ah sweet, too sweet to me, my sweet, I know
    Love, sleep, and death go to the sweet same tune;
Hold my hair fast, and kiss me through it soon.
    Ah God, ah God, that day should be so soon.

GREEN

The dawn was apple-green,
   The sky was green wine held up in the sun,
The moon was a golden petal between.

She opened her eyes, and green
   They shone, clear like flowers undone
For the first time, now for the first time seen.

In summer's heat and mid-time of the day
To rest my limbs upon a bed I lay,
One window shut, the other open stood,
Which gave such light as twinkles in a wood,
Like twilight glimpse at setting of the sun
Or night being past, and yet not day begun.
Such light to shamefaced maidens must be shown,
Where they may sport, and seem to be unknown.
Then came Corinna in a long loose gown,
Her white neck hid with tresses hanging down:
Resembling fair Semiramis going to bed
Or Laïs of a thousand wooers sped.
I snatched her gown, being thin, the harm was small,
Yet strived she to be covered therewithal.
And striving thus as one that would be cast,
Betrayed herself, and yielded at the last.
Stark naked as she stood before mine eye,
Not one wen in her body could I spy.

What arms and shoulders did I touch and see,
How apt her breasts were to be pressed by me?
How smooth a belly under her waist saw I?
How large a leg, and what a lusty thigh?
To leave the rest, all liked me passing well,
I clinged her naked body, down she fell,
Judge you the rest: being tired she bad me kiss,
Jove send me more such afternoons as this.

MEETING AT NIGHT

I

The grey sea and the long black land;
And the yellow half-moon large and low;
And the startled little waves that leap
In fiery ringlets from their sleep,
As I gain the cove with pushing prow,
And quench its speed i' the slushy sand.

II

Then a mile of warm sea-scented beach;
Three fields to cross till a farm appears;
A tap at the pane, the quick sharp scratch
And blue spurt of a lighted match,
And a voice less loud, thro' its joys and fears,
Than the two hearts beating each to each!

ROBERT BROWNING (1812–1889)   121

HOW MANY KISSES

How many kisses satisfy,
How many are enough and more,
You ask me, Lesbia. I reply,
As many as the Libyan sands
Sprinkling the Cyrenaic shore
Where silphium grows, between the places
Where old King Battus's tomb stands
And Jupiter Ammon has his shrine
In Siwa's sweltering oasis;
As many as the stars above
That in the dead of midnight shine
Upon men's secrecies of love.
When he has all those kisses, mad-
Hungry Catullus will have had
Enough to slake his appetite –
So many that sharp eyes can't tell
The number, and the tongues of spite
Are too confused to form a spell.

CATULLUS (*c.* 84–*c.* 54 BC),
TRANS. JAMES MICHIE

FOR AN AMOROUS LADY

*'Most mammals like caresses, in the sense in which we
usually take the word, whereas other creatures, even
tame snakes, prefer giving to receiving them.'*
                    FROM A NATURAL-HISTORY BOOK

The pensive gnu, the staid aardvark,
Accept caresses in the dark;
The bear, equipped with paw and snout,
Would rather take than dish it out.
But snakes, both poisonous and garter,
In love are never known to barter;
The worm, though dank, is sensitive:
His noble nature bids him *give*.

But you, my dearest, have a soul
Encompassing fish, flesh, and fowl.
When amorous arts we would pursue,
You can, with pleasure, bill *or* coo.
You are, in truth, one in a million,
At once mammalian and reptilian.

THEODORE ROETHKE (1908–1963)   123

ANOTHER FAN
(Mademoiselle Mallarmé's)

Dear dreamer, help me to take off
Into my pathless, pure delight,
By always holding in your glove
My wing, a thin pretence of flight.

A freshness as of twilight brushes
Against you as you flutter me,
And each imprisoned wing-beat pushes
Back the horizon tenderly.

It's dizzying: shivers run through space
Like an enormous kiss, which, mad
At being born for no one's face,
Can not discharge, nor yet subside.

Don't you feel heaven is shy? It slips,
Blushing, a piece of laughter stifled,
Down by the corner of your lips
To hide in my concerted fold.

This sceptre rules the banks of rose
And pools of evening's golden mire,
This flying whiteness that you close
And land beside a bracelet's fire.

124   STÉPHANE MALLARMÉ (1842–1898),
      TRANS. ALISTAIR ELLIOT

PLUCKING THE RUSHES
A boy and a girl are sent to gather rushes for thatching

Green rushes with red shoots,
Long leaves bending to the wind –
You and I in the same boat
Plucking rushes at the Five Lakes.

We started at dawn from the orchid-island:
We rested under elms till noon.
You and I plucking rushes
Had not plucked a handful when night came!

THE GOOD MORROW

I wonder by my troth, what thou and I
    Did, till we loved? were we not weaned till then?
But sucked on country pleasures, childishly?
    Or snorted we i'the seven sleepers' den?
'Twas so; But this, all pleasures fancies be.
If ever any beauty I did see,
Which I desired, and got, 'twas but a dream of thee.

And now good morrow to our waking souls,
    Which watch not one another out of fear;
For love, all love of other sights controls,
    And makes one little room, an everywhere.
Let sea-discoverers to new worlds have gone,
Let maps to others, worlds on worlds have shown,
Let us possess our world, each hath one, and is one.

My face in thine eye, thine in mine appears,
    And true plain hearts do in the faces rest,
Where can we find two better hemispheres
    Without sharp North, without declining West?
Whatever dies, was not mixed equally;
If our two loves be one, or, thou and I
Love so alike, that none do slacken, none can die.

A POMEGRANATE

A pomegranate just splitting, a peach just furry,
a fig with wrinkled flesh and juicy bottom,
a purple cluster (thick-berried well of wine),
nuts just skinned from their green peelings – these
the guardian of the fruit lays here for Priapus:
for this single shaft in the wilds, the seed of trees.

DIODOROS ZONAS (*c.* 100 BC),
TRANS. ALISTAIR ELLIOT

From ODES, BOOK THREE, 15
'Love and Gold'

I

A Tower of Brass, one would have said,
And Locks, and Bolts, and Iron Bars,
Might have preserv'd one innocent Maiden-head.
The jealous Father thought he well might spare
All further jealous Care.
And, as he walk'd, t'himself alone he smiled,
To think how Venus' Arts he had beguil'd;
  And when he slept, his Rest was deep:
  But Venus laugh'd, to see and hear him sleep:
   She taught the am'rous Jove
   A magical Receipt in Love,
Which arm'd him stronger, and which help'd him more,
Than all his Thunder did, and his Almightyship before.

II

She taught him Love's Elixir, by which Art
His Godhead into Gold he did convert;
    No Guards did then his Passage stay,
    He pass'd with Ease, Gold was the Word;
Subtle as Light'ning, bright, and quick, and fierce,
Gold thro' Doors and Walls did pierce;
And as that works sometimes upon the Sword,
    Melted the Maidenhead away,
    Ev'n in the secret Scabbard where it lay.
    The prudent Macedonian King,
    To blow up Towns a Golden Mine did spring;
    He broke thro' Gates with this Petarr,
'Tis the great Art of Peace, the Engine 'tis of War;
And Fleets and Armies follow it afar;
The Ensign 'tis at Land: and 'tis the Seaman's Star.

HORACE (65–8 BC),   129
TRANS. ABRAHAM COWLEY (1618–1687)

HE WHISPERS

He whispers: 'I'm not sorry
For loving you this way –
Either be mine alone
Or I will kill you.'
It buzzes around me like a gadfly,
Incessantly, day after day,
This same boring argument,
Your black jealousy.
Grief smothers – but not fatally,
The wide wind dries my tears
And cheerfulness begins to soothe,
To smooth out this troubled heart.

OUR KISSES

Our kisses
      Rhodope
let us steal,
      and slip
with furtive ease
like burglars
      into bed.

To cheat the eyes
      of stern
leering prudes
adds honey to
      love's cup.

WITH HOW SAD STEPS

With how sad steps, O moon, thou climb'st the skies!
How silently, and with how wan a face!
What! may it be that even in heavenly place
That busy archer his sharp arrows tries?
Sure, if that long-with-love-acquainted eyes
Can judge of love, thou feel'st a lover's case:
I read it in thy looks; thy languished grace
To me, that feel the like, thy state descries.
Then, even of fellowship, O Moon, tell me,
Is constant love deemed there but want of wit?
Are beauties there as proud as here they be?
Do they above love to be loved, and yet
    Those lovers scorn whom that love doth possess?
    Do they call 'virtue' there – ungratefulness?

WHO SO LIST TO HUNT

Who so list to hunt, I know where is an hind,
But as for me, helas, I may no more:
The vain travail hath wearied me so sore,
I am of them that farthest cometh behind;
Yet may I by no means my wearied mind
Draw from the deer: but as she fleeth afore,
Fainting I follow, I leave off therefore,
Since in a net I seek to hold the wind.
Who list her hunt, I put him out of doubt,
As well as I may spend his time in vain:
And, graven with diamonds, in letters plain,
There is written, her fair neck round about:
Noli me tangere, for Caesar's I am,
And wild for to hold, though I seem tame.

I LOVED YOU

I loved you; even now I may confess,
   Some embers of my love their fire retain;
But do not let it cause you more distress,
   I do not want to sadden you again.
Hopeless and tonguetied, yet I loved you dearly
   With pangs the jealous and timid know;
So tenderly I loved you, so sincerely,
   I pray God grant another love you so.

134 ALEXANDER PUSHKIN (1799–1837),
    TRANS. R. M. HEWITT

THE LION IN LOVE
To Mademoiselle de Sévigné

Mademoiselle – goddess instead –
In whom the Graces find a school
Although you are more beautiful,
Even if with averted head,
Might you not be entertained
By a tale that is unadorned –
Hearing with no more than a quiver
Of a lion whom Love knew how to conquer.
Love is a curious mastery,
In name alone a felicity.
Better know of than know the thing.
If too personal and thus trespassing,
I'm saying what may seem to you an offense,
A fable could not offend your ear.
This one, assured of your lenience,
Attests its devotion embodied here,
And kneels in sworn obedience.

Before their speech was obstructed,
Lions or such as were attracted
To young girls, sought an alliance.
Why not? since as paragons of puissance,
They were at that time knightly fellows
Of mettle and intelligence
Adorned by manes like haloes.

The point of the preamble follows.
A lion – one in a multitude –
Met in a meadow as he fared,
A shepherdess for whom he cared.
He sought to win her if he could,
Though the father would have preferred
A less ferocious son-in-law.
To consent undoubtedly was hard;
Fear meant that the alternate was barred.
Moreover, refuse and he foresaw
That some fine day the two might explain
Clandestine marriage as the chain
That fettered the lass, bewitched beyond cure,
By fashions conducive to hauteur,
And a fancy that shaggy shoulder fur
Made her willful lover handsomer.
The father with despair choked down,
Said though at heart constrained to frown,

'The child is a dainty one; better wait;
You might let your claw points scratch her
When your heavy forepaws touch her.
You could if not too importunate,
Have your claws clipped. And there in front,
See that your teeth are filed blunt,
Because a kiss might be enjoyed
By you the more, I should think,
If my daughter were not forced to shrink
Because improvidently annoyed.'
The enthralled animal mellowed,
His mind's eye having been shuttered.
Without teeth or claws it followed
That the fortress was shattered.
Dogs were loosed; defenses were gone:
The consequence was slight resistance.

Love, ah Love, when your slipknot's drawn,
We can but say, 'Farewell, good sense.'

THE FOLLY OF BEING COMFORTED

One that is ever kind said yesterday:
'Your well-beloved's hair has threads of grey,
And little shadows come about her eyes;
Time can but make it easier to be wise
Though now it seems impossible, and so
All that you need is patience.'
                Heart cries, 'No,
I have not a crumb of comfort, not a grain.
Time can but make her beauty over again:
Because of that great nobleness of hers
The fire that stirs about her, when she stirs,
Burns but more clearly. O she had not these ways
When all the wild summer was in her gaze.'

O heart! O heart! if she'd but turn her head,
You'd know the folly of being comforted.

QUICK AND BITTER

The end was quick and bitter.
Slow and sweet was the time between us,
Slow and sweet were the nights
When my hands did not touch one another in despair
But with the love of your body
Which came between them.

And when I entered into you
It seemed then that great happiness
Could be measured with the precision
Of sharp pain. Quick and bitter.

Slow and sweet were the nights.
Now is as bitter and grinding as sand –
'We shall be sensible' and similar curses.

And as we stray further from love
We multiply the words,
Words and sentences long and orderly.
Had we remained together
We could have become a silence.

YEHUDA AMICHAI (1924–   ),
TRANS. ASSIA GUTMANN

THE YOUNG BLOODS

The young bloods come round less often now,
Pelting your shutters and making a row
And robbing your beauty sleep. Now the door
Clings lovingly close to the jamb – though, before,

It used to move on its hinge pretty fast.
Those were the days – and they're almost past –
When lovers stood out all night long crying,
'Lydia, wake up! Save me! I'm dying!'

Soon your time's coming to be turned down
And to feel the scorn of the men about town –
A cheap hag haunting alley places
On moonless nights when the wind from Thrace is

Rising and raging, and so is the fire
In your raddled loins, the brute desire
That drives the mothers of horses mad.
You'll be lonely then and complain how sad

That the gay young boys enjoy the sheen
Of ivy best or the darker green
Of myrtle: dry old leaves they send
As a gift to the east wind, winter's friend.

140   HORACE (65–8 BC),
       TRANS. JAMES MICHIE

THE MIRABEAU BRIDGE

Under the Mirabeau bridge the Seine
    Flows with our loves;
Must I remember once again
Joy followed always after pain?
    Night may come and clock may sound,
    Within your shadow I am bound.

Clasp hand in hand, keep face to face,
    Whilst here below
The bridge formed by our arms' embrace
The waters of our endless longing pass.
    Night may come and clock may sound,
    Within your shadow I am bound.

And like this stream our passions flow,
    Our love goes by;
The violence hope dare not show
Follows time's beat which now falls slow.
    Night may come and clock may sound,
    Within your shadow I am bound.

The days move on; but still we strain
   Back towards time past;
Still to the waters of the Seine
We bend to catch the echo gone.
   Night may come and clock may sound,
   Within your shadow I am bound.

142   GUILLAUME APOLLINAIRE (1880–1918),
      TRANS. QUENTIN STEVENSON

I HID MY LOVE

I hid my love when young till I
Couldn't bear the buzzing of a fly;
I hid my love to my despite
Till I could not bear to look at light:
I dare not gaze upon her face
But left her memory in each place;
Where'er I saw a wild flower lie
I kissed and bade my love good-bye.

I met her in the greenest dells,
Where dewdrops pearl the wood bluebells;
The lost breeze kissed her bright blue eye,
The bee kissed and went singing by,
A sunbeam found a passage there,
A gold chain round her neck so fair;
As secret as the wild bee's song
She lay there all the summer long.

I hid my love in field and town
Till e'en the breeze would knock me down;
The bees seemed singing ballads o'er,
The fly's bass turned a lion's roar;
And even silence found a tongue,
To haunt me all the summer long;
The riddle nature could not prove
Was nothing else but secret love.

WHEN IN DISGRACE

When in disgrace with fortune and men's eyes,
I all alone beweep my outcast state,
And trouble deaf heaven with my bootless cries,
And look upon myself, and curse my fate,
Wishing me like to one more rich in hope,
Featur'd like him, like him with friends possess'd,
Desiring this man's art, and that man's scope,
With what I most enjoy contented least;
Yet in these thoughts myself almost despising,
Haply I think on thee, and then my state,
Like to the lark at break of day arising
From sullen earth, sings hymns at heaven's gate;
    For thy sweet love rememb'red such wealth brings,
    That then I scorn to change my state with kings.

VOBISCUM EST IOPE

When thou must home to shades of underground,
And there arrived, a new admirèd guest,
The beauteous spirits do engirt thee round,
White Iope, blithe Helen, and the rest,
To hear the stories of thy finished love
From that smooth tongue whose music hell can move;

Then wilt thou speak of banqueting delights,
Of masques and revels which sweet youth did make,
Of tourneys and great challenges of knights,
And all these triumphs for thy beauty's sake:
When thou hast told these honours done to thee,
Then tell, O tell, how thou didst murder me!

AH, YOU THOUGHT

Ah – you thought I'd be the type
You could forget,
And that praying and sobbing, I'd throw myself
Under the hooves of a bay.

Or I would beg from the witches
Some kind of root in charmed water
And send you a terrible gift –
My intimate, scented handkerchief.

Damned if I will. Neither by glance nor by groan
Will I touch your cursed soul,
But I vow to you by the garden of angels,
By the miraculous icon I vow
And by the fiery passion of our nights –
I will never return to you.

ONE PERFECT ROSE

A single flow'r he sent me, since we met.
    All tenderly his messenger he chose;
Deep-hearted, pure, with scented dew still wet –
    One perfect rose.

I knew the language of the floweret;
    'My fragile leaves,' it said, 'his heart enclose.'
Love long has taken for his amulet
    One perfect rose.

Why is it no one ever sent me yet
    One perfect limousine, do you suppose?
Ah no, it's always just my luck to get
    One perfect rose.

TH'EXPENSE OF SPIRIT

Th'expense of spirit in a waste of shame
Is lust in action, and till action, lust
Is perjur'd, murd'rous, bloody, full of blame,
Savage, extreme, rude, cruel, not to trust;
Enjoy'd no sooner but despised straight;
Past reason hunted, and no sooner had,
Past reason hated as a swallowed bait,
On purpose laid to make the taker mad;
Mad in pursuit and in possession so;
Had, having, and in quest, to have, extreme;
A bliss in proof, and prov'd, a very woe;
Before a joy propos'd, behind a dream,
    All this the world well knows yet none knows well;
    To shun the heaven that leads men to this hell.

DOING

Doing, a filthy pleasure is, and short;
And done, we straight repent us of the sport:
Let us not then rush blindly on unto it,
Like lustful beasts, that only know to do it:
For lust will languish, and that heat decay.
But thus, thus, keeping endless holiday,
Let us together closely lie and kiss,
There is no labour, nor no shame in this;
This hath pleased, doth please, and long will please; never
Can this decay, but is beginning ever.

150 PETRONIUS (1ST CENTURY AD),
        TRANS. BEN JONSON (1572/3–1637)

FIDELITY AND
INCONSTANCY

LULLABY

Beloved, may your sleep be sound
That have found it where you fed.
What were all the world's alarms
To mighty Paris when he found
Sleep upon a golden bed
That first dawn in Helen's arms?

Sleep, beloved, such a sleep
As did that wild Tristram know
When, the potion's work being done,
Roe could run or doe could leap
Under oak and beechen bough,
Roe could leap or doe could run;

Such a sleep and sound as fell
Upon Eurotas' grassy bank
When the holy bird, that there
Accomplished his predestined will,
From the limbs of Leda sank
But not from her protecting care.

LULLABY

Lay your sleeping head, my love,
Human on my faithless arm;
Time and fevers burn away
Individual beauty from
Thoughtful children, and the grave
Proves the child ephemeral:
But in my arms till break of day
Let the living creature lie,
Mortal, guilty, but to me
The entirely beautiful.

Soul and body have no bounds:
To lovers as they lie upon
Her tolerant enchanted slope
In their ordinary swoon,
Grave the vision Venus sends
Of supernatural sympathy,
Universal love and hope;
While an abstract insight wakes
Among the glaciers and the rocks
The hermit's sensual ecstasy.

Certainty, fidelity
On the stroke of midnight pass
Like vibrations of a bell
And fashionable madmen raise
Their pedantic boring cry;
Every farthing of the cost,
All the dreaded cards foretell,
Shall be paid, but from this night
Not a whisper, not a thought,
Not a kiss nor look be lost.

Beauty, midnight, vision dies:
Let the winds of dawn that blow
Softly round your dreaming head
Such a day of sweetness show
Eye and knocking heart may bless,
Find the mortal world enough;
Noons of dryness see you fed
By the involuntary powers,
Nights of insult let you pass
Watched by every human love.

W. H. AUDEN (1907–1973)

DEAD STILL

Now, with your palms on the blades of my shoulders,
Let us embrace:
Let there be only your lips' breath on my face,
Only, behind our backs, the plunge of rollers.

Our backs, which like two shells in moonlight shine,
Are shut behind us now;
We lie here huddled, listening brow to brow,
Like life's twin formula or double sign.

In folly's world-wide wind
Our shoulders shield from the weather
The calm we now beget together,
Like a flame held between hand and hand.

Does each cell have a soul within it?
If so, fling open all your little doors,
And all your souls shall flutter like the linnet
In the cages of my pores.

Nothing is hidden that shall not be known.
Yet by no storm of scorn shall we
Be pried from this embrace, and left alone
Like muted shells forgetful of the sea.

Meanwhile, O load of stress and bother,
Lie on the shells of our backs in a great heap:
It will but press us closer, one to the other.

We are asleep.

ANDREI VOZNESENSKY (1933–   ),   157
TRANS. RICHARD WILBUR (1921–   )

LOVE AND SLEEP

Lying asleep between the strokes of night
   I saw my love lean over my sad bed,
   Pale as the duskiest lily's leaf or head,
Smooth-skinned and dark, with bare throat made to bite,
Too wan for blushing and too warm for white,
   But perfect-coloured without white or red.
   And her lips opened amorously, and said –
I wist not what, saving one word – Delight.

And all her face was honey to my mouth,
   And all her body pasture to mine eyes;
     The long lithe arms and hotter hands than fire,
The quivering flanks, hair smelling of the south,
   The bright light feet, the splendid supple thighs
     And glittering eyelids of my soul's desire.

SHE TELLS HER LOVE WHILE HALF ASLEEP

She tells her love while half asleep,
In the dark hours,
With half-words whispered low:
As Earth stirs in her winter sleep
And puts out grass and flowers
Despite the snow,
Despite the falling snow.

WHEN I HEARD AT THE CLOSE OF THE DAY

When I heard at the close of the day how my name had
    been receiv'd with plaudits in the capitol, still it was
    not a happy night for me that follow'd,
And else when I carous'd, or when my plans were
    accomplish'd, still I was not happy,
But the day when I rose at dawn from the bed of perfect
    health, refresh'd, singing, inhaling the ripe breath of
    autumn,
When I saw the full moon in the west grow pale and
    disappear in the morning light,
When I wander'd alone over the beach, and undressing
    bathed, laughing with the cool waters, and saw the
    sun rise,
And when I thought how my dear friend my lover was
    on his way coming, O then I was happy,
O then each breath tasted sweeter, and all that day my
    food nourish'd me more, and the beautiful day pass'd
    well,
And the next came with equal joy, and with the next at
    evening came my friend,
And that night while all was still I heard the waters roll
    slowly continually up the shores,
I heard the hissing rustle of the liquid and sands as
    directed to me whispering to congratulate me,

For the one I love most lay sleeping by me under the
same cover in the cool night,
In the stillness in the autumn moonbeams his face was
inclined toward me,
And his arm lay lightly around my breast – and that
night I was happy.

THE ECSTASY

Where, like a pillow on a bed,
    A pregnant bank swelled up, to rest
The violet's reclining head,
    Sat we two, one another's best.

Our hands were firmly cemented
    With a fast balm, which thence did spring;
Our eye-beams twisted, and did thread
    Our eyes upon one double string;

So to entergraft our hands, as yet
    Was all our means to make us one.
And pictures on our eyes to get
    Was all our propagation.

As 'twixt two equal armies, Fate
    Suspends uncertain victory,
Our souls (which to advance their state
    Were gone out) hung 'twixt her and me.

And whilst our souls negotiate there,
    We like sepulchral statues lay;
All day the same our postures were,
    And we said nothing all the day.

If any, so by love refined
    That he soul's language understood,
And by good love were grown all mind,
    Within convenient distance stood,

He (though he knew not which soul spake,
    Because both meant, both spake the same)
Might thence a new concoction take,
    And part far purer than he came,

This ectasy doth unperplex
    (We said) and tell us what we love,
We see by this, it was not sex,
    We see, we saw not what did move:

But as all several souls contain
    Mixture of things, they know not what,
Love these mixed souls doth mix again,
    And makes both one, each this and that.

A single violet transplant,
    The strength, the colour, and the size,
(All which before was poor and scant)
    Redoubles still, and multiplies.

When love with one another so
    Interinanimates two souls,
That abler soul, which thence doth flow,
    Defects of loneliness controls.

We then, who are this new soul, know
    Of what we are composed, and made,
For the atomies of which we grow
    Are souls, whom no change can invade.

But, O alas! so long, so far
    Our bodies why do we forbear?
They are ours, though they are not we; we are
    The intelligences, they the sphere.

We owe them thanks, because they thus
    Did us, to us, at first convey,
Yielded their forces, sense, to us,
    Nor are dross to us, but allay.

On man heaven's influence works not so,
    But that it first imprints the air;
So soul into the soul may flow,
    Though it to body first repair.

As our blood labours to beget
   Spirits, as like souls as it can;
Because such fingers need to knit
   That subtle knot, which makes us man;

So must pure lovers' souls descend
   To affections, and to faculties,
Which sense may reach and apprehend,
   Else a great Prince in prison lies.

To our bodies turn we then, that so
   Weak men on love revealed may look;
Love's mysteries in souls do grow,
   But yet the body is his book.

And if some lover, such as we,
   Have heard this dialogue of one,
Let him still mark us, he shall see
   Small change, when we're to bodies gone.

JOHN DONNE (?1572–1631)   165

From THE PRINCESS

'Now sleeps the crimson petal, now the white;
Nor waves the cypress in the palace walk;
Nor winks the gold fin in the porphyry font:
The fire-fly wakens: waken thou with me.

Now droops the milkwhite peacock like a ghost,
And like a ghost she glimmers on to me.

Now lies the Earth all Danaë to the stars,
And all thy heart lies open unto me.

Now slides the silent meteor on, and leaves
A shining furrow, as thy thoughts in me.

Now folds the lily all her sweetness up,
And slips into the bosom of the lake:
So fold thyself, my dearest, thou, and slip
Into my bosom and be lost in me.'

NO ONE SO MUCH AS YOU

No one so much as you
Loves this my clay,
Or would lament as you
Its dying day.

You know me through and through
Though I have not told,
And though with what you know
You are not bold.

None ever was so fair
As I thought you:
Not a word can I bear
Spoken against you.

All that I ever did
For you seemed coarse
Compared with what I hid
Nor put in force.

My eyes scarce dare meet you
Lest they should prove
I but respond to you
And do not love.

We look and understand,
We cannot speak
Except in trifles and
Words the most weak.

For I at most accept
Your love, regretting
That is all: I have kept
Only a fretting

That I could not return
All that you gave
And could not ever burn
With the love you have,

Till sometimes it did seem
Better it were
Never to see you more
Than linger here

With only gratitude
Instead of love –
A pine in solitude
Cradling a dove.

IT IS AT MOMENTS AFTER I HAVE DREAMED

it is at moments after i have dreamed
of the rare entertainment of your eyes,
when (being fool to fancy) i have deemed

with your peculiar mouth my heart made wise;
at moments when the glassy darkness holds

the genuine apparition of your smile
(it was through tears always) and silence moulds
such strangeness as was mine a little while;

moments when my once more illustrious arms
are filled with fascination, when my breast
wears the intolerant brightness of your charms:

one pierced moment whiter than the rest

– turning from the tremendous lie of sleep
i watch the roses of the day grow deep.

E. E. CUMMINGS (1894–1962)   169

IN THE WOOD

The field was clouded with a lilac heat.
Through the wood rolled the darkness of cathedrals.
What in the world remained for them to kiss?
It was all theirs, like soft wax in their fingers.

This is the dream, – you do not sleep, but dream
you thirst for sleep, that there's a fellow dozing
and through his dream from underneath his eyelids
a pair of black suns break and burn his lashes.

Their beams flowed by. And iridescent beetles.
The glass of dragon-flies roamed over cheeks.
The wood was full of tiny scintillations,
as at the clockmaker's beneath his tweezers.

It seemed he slumbered to the figures' tick,
while high above his head in harshest amber
they place in ether strictly tested clocks
and regulate them to the change of heat.

They shift them round about and shake the needles
and scatter shadow, swing and bore a place
for the tall masts' gloom, that's climbed into the day's
fatigue and lies across the deep blue dial.

It seemed that ancient joys were flying over,
sunset of dreams once more embraced the wood.
But happy people do not watch the clocks;
it seems they only lie in pairs and sleep.

BORIS PASTERNAK (1890–1960)   171
TRANS. J. M. COWEN

THE RIVER-MERCHANT'S WIFE:
A LETTER

While my hair was still cut straight across my forehead
I played about the front gate, pulling flowers.
You came by on bamboo stilts, playing horse,
You walked about my seat, playing with blue plums.
And we went on living in the village of Chokan:
Two small people, without dislike or suspicion.

At fourteen I married My Lord you.
I never laughed, being bashful.
Lowering my head, I looked at the wall.
Called to, a thousand times, I never looked back.

At fifteen I stopped scowling,
I desired my dust to be mingled with yours
For ever and for ever and for ever.
Why should I climb the look out?

At sixteen you departed,
You went into far Ku-to-yen, by the river of swirling
        eddies,
And you have been gone five months.
The monkeys make sorrowful noise overhead

You dragged your feet when you went out.
By the gate now, the moss is grown, the different mosses,
Too deep to clear them away!
The leaves fall early this autumn, in wind.
The paired butterflies are already yellow with August
Over the grass in the West garden;
They hurt me. I grow older.
If you are coming down through the narrows of the
        river Kiang,
Please let me know beforehand,
And I will come out to meet you
                As far as Cho-fu-Sa.

LI PO (701–762),   173
TRANS. EZRA POUND (1885–1972)

WILD PEACHES

I

When the world turns completely upside down
You say we'll emigrate to the Eastern Shore
Aboard a river-boat from Baltimore;
We'll live among wild peach trees, miles from town,
You'll wear a coonskin cap, and I a gown
Homespun, dyed butternut's dark gold colour.
Lost, like your lotus-eating ancestor,
We'll swim in milk and honey till we drown.

The winter will be short, the summer long,
The autumn amber-hued, sunny and hot,
Tasting of cider and of scuppernong;
All seasons sweet, but autumn best of all.
The squirrels in their silver fur will fall
Like falling leaves, like fruit, before your shot.

II

The autumn frosts will lie upon the grass
Like bloom on grapes of purple-brown and gold.
The misted early mornings will be cold;
The little puddles will be roofed with glass.
The sun, which burns from copper into brass,
Melts these at noon, and makes the boys unfold
Their knitted mufflers; full as they can hold,
Fat pockets dribble chestnuts as they pass.

Peaches grow wild, and pigs can live in clover;
A barrel of salted herrings lasts a year;
The spring begins before the winter's over.
By February you may find the skins
Of garter snakes and water moccasins
Dwindled and harsh, dead-white and cloudy-clear.

MAN AND WIFE

Tamed by Miltown, we lie on Mother's bed;
the rising sun in war paint dyes us red;
in broad daylight her gilded bed-posts shine,
abandoned, almost Dionysian.
At last the trees are green on Marlborough Street,
blossoms on our magnolia ignite
the morning with their murderous five days' white.
All night I've held your hand,
as if you had
a fourth time faced the kingdom of the mad –
its hackneyed speech, its homicidal eye –
and dragged me home alive. . . . Oh my *Petite*,
clearest of all God's creatures, still all air and nerve:
you were in your twenties, and I,
once hand on glass
and heart in mouth,
outdrank the Rahvs in the heat
of Greenwich Village, fainting at your feet –
too boiled and shy
and poker-faced to make a pass,
while the shrill verve
of your invective scorched the traditional South.

Now twelve years later, you turn your back.
Sleepless, you hold
your pillow to your hollows like a child,
your old-fashioned tirade –
loving, rapid, merciless –
breaks like the Atlantic Ocean on my head.

SHE HEARS THE STORM

There was a time in former years –
  While my roof-tree was his –
When I should have been distressed by fears
  At such a night as this!

I should have murmured anxiously,
  'The pricking rain strikes cold;
His road is bare of hedge or tree,
  And he is getting old.'

But now the fitful chimney-roar,
  The drone of Thorncombe trees,
The Froom in flood upon the moor,
  The mud of Mellstock Leaze,

The candle slanting sooty-wick'd,
  The thuds upon the thatch,
The eaves-drops on the window flicked,
  The clacking garden-hatch,

And what they mean to wayfarers,
  I scarcely heed or mind;
He has won that storm-tight roof of hers
  Which Earth grants all her kind.

WHERE DOES THIS TENDERNESS COME FROM?

Where does this tenderness come from?
These are not the – first curls I
have stroked slowly – and lips I
have known are – darker than yours

as stars rise often and go out again
(where does this tenderness come from?)
so many eyes have risen and died out
    in front of these eyes of mine.

and yet no such song have
I heard in the darkness of night before,
(where does this tenderness come from?):
    here, on the ribs of the singer.

Where does this tenderness come from?
And what shall I do with it, young
sly singer, just passing by?
Your lashes are – longer than anyone's.

MARINA TSVETAEVA (1892–1941),   179
TRANS. ELAINE FEINSTEIN

I, THROUGH ALL CHANCES
To Ausonius

I, through all chances that are given to mortals,
    And through all fates that be,
So long as this close prison shall contain me,
    Yea, though a world shall sunder me and thee,

Thee shall I hold, in every fibre woven,
    Not with dumb lips, nor with averted face
Shall I behold thee, in my mind embrace thee,
    Instant and present, thou, in every place.

Yea, when the prison of this flesh is broken,
    And from the earth I shall have gone my way,
Wheresoe'er in the wide universe I stay me,
    There shall I bear thee, as I do to-day.

Think not the end, that from my body frees me,
    Breaks and unshackles from my love to thee;
Triumphs the soul above its house in ruin,
    Deathless, begot of immortality.

Still must she keep her senses and affections,
    Hold them as dear as life itself to be.
Could she choose death, then might she choose
      forgetting:
    Living, remembering, to eternity.

180   PAULINUS OF NOLA (353–431),
      TRANS. HELEN WADDELL (1889–1965)

CAPE MOOTCH

The mind is stifled. The horizon's
somehow tobacco brown, like thoughts.
From the mills you see the fishing village,
its stoops of war and its grey sails.

What makes her wait there, spoil the picture
of washtubs, crab-claws, spare mill sails,
filming with slime of useless tears
the last glint on the ugly fish-heads?

Oh, and an hour there like a pebble
springs off the shallows, skims the bay.
Oh, it's not sinking. No, it's there still
and it's tobacco brown, like thoughts.

Shall I see her again to-day, then?
There's one hour to the train. That's all.
But that one hour's held by the apathy
of sea, of rumbling storm, of hell.

BORIS PASTERNAK (1890–1960),   181
TRANS. J. M. COWEN

MANY IN AFTERTIMES

Vien dietro a me e lascia dir le genti. – DANTE.
Contando i casi della vita nostra. – PETRARCA.

Many in aftertimes will say of you
   'He loved her' – while of me what will they say?
   Not that I loved you more than just in play,
For fashion's sake as idle women do.
Even let them prate; who know not what we knew
   Of love and parting in exceeding pain.
   Of parting hopeless here to meet again,
Hopeless on earth, and heaven is out of view.
But by my heart of love laid bare to you.
   My love that you can make not void nor vain,
Love that foregoes you but to claim anew
     Beyond this passage of the gate of death,
   I charge you at the Judgment make it plain
     My love of you was life and not a breath.

I LOVED YOU FIRST

Poca favilla gran fiamma seconda. – DANTE.
Ogni altra cosa, ogni pensier va fore,
E sol ivi con voi rimansi amore. – PETRARCA.

I loved you first: but afterwards your love
   Outsoaring mine, sang such a loftier song
As drowned the friendly cooings of my dove.
   Which owes the other most? my love was long,
   And yours one moment seemed to wax more
       strong;
I loved and guessed at you, you construed me
And loved me for what might or might not be –
   Nay, weights and measures do us both a wrong.
For verily love knows not 'mine' or 'thine;'
   With separate 'I' and 'thou' free love has done,
    For one is both and both are one in love:
Rich love knows nought of 'thine that is not
       mine;'
   Both have the strength and both the length
    thereof,
   Both of us, of the love which makes us one.

NEVER SUCH LOVE

Twined together and, as is customary,
For words of rapture groping, they
'Never such love,' swore, 'ever before was!'
Contrast with all loves that had failed or staled
Registered their own as love indeed.

And was this not to blab idly
The heart's fated inconstancy?
Better in love to seal the love-sure lips,
For truly love was before words were,
And no word given, no word broken.

When the name 'love' is uttered
(Love, the near-honourable malady
With which in greed and haste they
Each other do infect and curse)
Or, worse, is written down . . .

Wise after the event, by love withered,
A 'never more!' most frantically
Sorrow and shame would proclaim
Such as, they'd swear, never before were:
True lovers even in this.

LOVE AND LIFE

All my past life is mine no more;
    The flying hours are gone,
Like transitory dreams given o'er
Whose images are kept in store
    By memory alone.

Whatever is to come is not:
    How can it then be mine?
The present moment's all my lot,
And that, as fast as it is got,
    Phyllis, is wholly thine.

Then talk not of inconstancy,
    False hearts, and broken vows;
If I, by miracle, can be
This livelong minute true to thee,
    'Tis all that heaven allows.

PROBLEMS OF GENDER

Circling the Sun, at a respectful distance,
Earth remains warmed, not roasted; but the Moon
Circling the Earth, at a disdainful distance,
Will drive men lunatic (should they defy her)
With seeds of wintry love, not sown for spite.

Mankind, so far, continues undecided
On the Sun's gender – grammars disagree –
As on the Moon's. Should Moon be god, or goddess:
Drawing the tide, shepherding flocks of stars
That never show themselves by broad daylight?

Thus curious problems of propriety
Challenge all ardent lovers of each sex:
Which circles which at a respectful distance,
Or which, instead, at a disdainful distance?
And who controls the regal powers of night?

OH, WHEN I WAS IN LOVE

Oh, when I was in love with you,
    Then I was clean and brave,
And miles around the wonder grew
    How well did I behave.

And now the fancy passes by,
    And nothing will remain,
And miles around they'll say that I
    Am quite myself again.

AS LOVE AND I

As Love and I, late harbour'd in one inn,
With proverbs thus each other entertain:
In love there is no lack, thus I begin,
Fair words make fools, replieth he again;
Who spares to speak, doth spare to speed (quoth I),
As well (saith he) too forward, as too slow;
Fortune assists the boldest, I reply,
A hasty man (quoth he) ne'er wanted woe;
Labour is light, where love (quoth I) doth pay,
(Saith he) light burthen's heavy, if far born;
(Quoth I) the main lost, cast the bye away;
You have spun a fair thread, he replies in scorn.
  And having thus awhile each other thwarted,
  Fools as we met, so fools again we parted.

SHE WHO IS ALWAYS IN MY THOUGHTS

She who is always in my thoughts prefers
Another man, and does not think of me.
Yet he seeks for another's love, not hers;
And some poor girl is grieving for my sake.
     Why then, the devil take
Both her and him; and love; and her; and me.

BHARTṚHARI (5TH CENTURY),
TRANS. JOHN BROUGH

FRIDAY NIGHT

Love, the sole Goddess fit for swearing by,
Concedes us graciously the little lie:
The white lie, the half-lie, the lie corrective
Without which love's exchange might prove defective,
Confirming hazardous relationships
By kindly *maquillage* of Truth's pale lips.

This little lie was first told, so they say,
On the sixth day (Love's planetary day)
When, meeting her full-bosomed and half dressed,
Jove roared out suddenly: 'Hell take the rest!
Six hard days of Creation are enough' –
And clasped her to him, meeting no rebuff.

Next day he rested, and she rested too.
The busy little lie between them flew:
'If this be not perfection,' Love would sigh,
'Perfection is a great, black, thumping lie. . . .'
Endearments, kisses, grunts, and whispered oaths;
But were her thoughts on breakfast, or on clothes?

ABSENCE, ESTRANGEMENT AND PARTING

TO MRS M. A. UPON ABSENCE

'Tis now since I began to die
    Four months, yet still I gasping live;
Wrapp'd up in sorrow do I lie,
    Hoping, yet doubting a reprieve.
Adam from Paradise expell'd
Just such a wretched being held.

'Tis not thy love I fear to lose,
    That will in spite of absence hold;
But 'tis the benefit and use
    Is lost, as in imprison'd gold:
Which though the sum be ne'er so great,
Enriches nothing but conceit.

What angry star then governs me
    That I must feel a double smart,
Prisoner to fate as well as thee;
    Kept from thy face, link'd to thy heart?
Because my love all love excels,
Must my grief have no parallels?

Sapless and dead as Winter here
    I now remain, and all I see
Copies of my wild state appear,
    But I am their epitome.
Love me no more, for I am grown
Too dead and dull for thee to own.

TO THE BELOVED

Don't send me a dove,
Don't write me disquieting letters,
Don't make the March wind keen in my face.
Yesterday I entered green paradise,
Where there is peace for body and soul
Under a tent of the poplars' shadow.

And from here I see the little city,
The barracks and sentry boxes at the palace,
The yellow Chinese bridge above the ice.
For three hours you've been awaiting me – you waver,
But you cannot leave the porch
And you marvel, so many new stars.

As a gray squirrel, I will leap on the alder tree,
As a weasel, shy, I'll scurry by,
As a swan, I'll call to you,
So that it won't be terrible for the groom
To wait in the whirling blue snow
For his dead bride.

ANNA AKHMATOVA (1889–1966),
TRANS. JUDITH HEMSCHEMEYER

IN THE MOONLIT CHAMBER

In the moonlit chamber, always she thinks of him.
Soft wisps of silken willows, languor in the air of
    spring.
  Verdant were the grasses beyond the gate;
  At their parting, she heard the horses neigh.

  Draperies patterned of gold kingfishers;
  Within, fragrant candle melts in tears.
  Falling petals, the morning plaint of the cuckoo,
  Green-gauze windows – fragments of an illusive
    dream.

196 WÊN T'ING-YÜN (?813–870),
    TRANS. WILLIAM R. SCHULTZ

THE FOOTSTEPS

Your steps, born of my silence here,
Process with slow, religious tread,
Dumbly and icily, to where
I lie awake, on watch, in bed.

Pure person, shade of deity,
Your steps, held back, are doubly sweet.
God! – all the gifts I could foresee
Are coming now on those bare feet!

If you advance your lips to make
A peace with hunger, and to press
The inhabitant of my thoughts to take
The thoughtful nourishment of a kiss,

Don't hurry with their tender dew,
Sweetness complete and incomplete;
For I have lived to wait for you:
My heart was your approaching feet.

PAUL VALÉRY (1871–1945),   197
TRANS. ALISTAIR ELLIOT

NEVERMORE

Memory, why torment me? Autumn skimmed
A struggling thrush through the dull air. The sun
Darted a colourless wand of light upon
The yellowing wood which thunders in the wind.

We were alone, and as we walked we dreamed,
Our hair and thoughts both flying in the breeze.
And then she turned to me her touching eyes:
'What was your loveliest day?' – her golden sound,

Her sweet voice, deep, with a fresh angelic ring.
A tactful smile was all I need reply,
And kissing her white hand – religiously.

– Oh, the first flowers – what a scent they have!
And what a charm breathes in the murmuring
Of the first *yes* that comes from lips you love!

198   PAUL VERLAINE (1844–1896)
      TRANS. ALISTAIR ELLIOT

SOMEWHERE OR OTHER

Somewhere or other there must surely be
    The face not seen, the voice not heard,
The heart that not yet – never yet – ah me!
    Made answer to my word.

Somewhere or other, may be near or far;
    Past land and sea, clean out of sight;
Beyond the wandering moon, beyond the star
    That tracks her night by night.

Somewhere or other, may be far or near;
    With just a wall, a hedge, between;
With just the last leaves of the dying year
    Fallen on a turf grown green.

FROM YOU HAVE I BEEN ABSENT
IN THE SPRING

From you have I been absent in the spring,
When proud-pied April, dressed in all his trim,
Hath put a spirit of youth in everything,
That heavy Saturn laughed and leaped with him.
Yet nor the lays of birds, nor the sweet smell
Of different flowers in odour and in hue,
Could make me any summer's story tell,
Or from their proud lap pluck them where they grew:
Nor did I wonder at the lily's white,
Nor praise the deep vermilion in the rose;
They were but sweet, but figures of delight,
Drawn after you, – you pattern of all those.
   Yet seem'd it winter still, and, you away,
   As with your shadow I with these did play.

TALKING IN BED

Talking in bed ought to be easiest,
Lying together there goes back so far,
An emblem of two people being honest.

Yet more and more time passes silently.
Outside, the wind's incomplete unrest
Builds and disperses clouds about the sky,

And dark towns heap up on the horizon.
None of this cares for us. Nothing shows why
At this unique distance from isolation

It becomes still more difficult to find
Words at once true and kind,
Or not untrue and not unkind.

REMEMBRANCE

They flee from me, that sometime did me seek
   With naked foot, stalking in my chamber.
I have seen them gentle, tame, and meek,
   That now are wild, and do not remember
   That sometime they put themselves in danger
      To take bread at my hand; and now they range
      Busily seeking with a continual change.

Thanked be fortune it hath been otherwise
   Twenty times better; but once, in special,
In thin array, after a pleasant guise,
   When her loose gown from her shoulders did fall,
   And she me caught in her arms long and small;
      Therewith all sweetly did me kiss,
      And softly said, 'Dear heart, how like you this?'

It was no dream: I lay broad waking:
   But all is turned, thorough my gentleness,
Into a strange fashion of forsaking;
   And I have leave to go of her goodness,
   And she also to use newfangleness.
      But since that I so kindly am served,
      I would fain know what she hath deserved.

EPISTLE TO MISS BLOUNT, ON HER LEAVING THE TOWN, AFTER THE CORONATION

As some fond virgin, whom her mother's care
Drags from the town to wholesome country air,
Just when she learns to roll a melting eye,
And hear a spark, yet think no danger nigh;
From the dear man unwilling she must sever,
Yet takes one kiss before she parts for ever:
Thus from the world fair Zephalinda flew,
Saw others happy, and with sighs withdrew;
Not that their pleasures caused her discontent,
She sighed not that They stayed, but that She went.

    She went, to plain-work, and to purling brooks,
Old-fashioned halls, dull aunts, and croaking rooks,
She went from Opera, park, assembly, play,
To morning walks, and prayers three hours a day;
To pass her time 'twixt reading and Bohea,
To muse, and spill her solitary tea,
Or o'er cold coffee trifle with the spoon,
Count the slow clock, and dine exact at noon;
Divert her eyes with pictures in the fire,
Hum half a tune, tell stories to the squire;
Up to her godly garret after seven,
There starve and pray, for that's the way to heaven.

    Some Squire, perhaps, you take a delight to rack;

Whose game is Whisk, whose treat a toast in sack,
Who visits with a gun, presents you birds,
Then gives a smacking buss, and cries – No words!
Or with his hound comes hollowing from the stable,
Makes love with nods, and knees beneath a table;
Whose laughs are hearty, tho' his jests are coarse,
And loves you best of all things – but his horse.

In some fair evening, on your elbow laid,
You dream of triumphs in the rural shade;
In pensive thought recall the fancied scene,
See Coronations rise on every green;
Before you pass th' imaginary sights
Of Lords, and Earls, and Dukes, and gartered Knights;
While the spread fan o'ershades your closing eyes;
Then give one flirt, and all the vision flies.
Thus vanish sceptres, coronets, and balls,
And leave you in lone woods, or empty walls.

So when your slave, at some dear, idle time,
(Not plagued with headaches, or the want of rhyme)
Stands in the streets, abstracted from the crew,
And while he seems to study, thinks of you:
Just when his fancy points your sprightly eyes,
Or sees the blush of soft Parthenia rise,
Gay pats my shoulder, and you vanish quite;
Streets, chairs, and coxcombs rush upon my sight;
Vexed to be still in town, I knit my brow,
Look sour, and hum a tune – as you may now.

I SAW MY LADY

I saw my Lady weep,
And Sorrow proud to be advanced so
In those fair eyes, where all perfections keep;
    Her face was full of woe,
But such a woe (believe me) as wins more hearts
Than mirth can do, with her enticing parts.

Sorrow was there made fair,
And Passion, wise; Tears, a delightful thing;
Silence, beyond all speech, a wisdom rare;
    She made her sighs to sing,
And all things with so sweet a sadness move;
As made my heart both grieve and love.

O Fairer than aught else
The world can shew, leave off, in time, to grieve,
Enough, enough! Your joyful look excels;
    Tears kill the heart, believe,
O strive not to be excellent in woe,
Which only breeds your beauty's overthrow.

I WISH I COULD REMEMBER

Era già l'ora che volge il desio. – DANTE.
Ricorro al tempo ch'io vi vidi prima. – PETRARCA.

I wish I could remember that first day,
    First hour, first moment of your meeting me,
    If bright or dim the season, it might be
Summer or Winter for aught I can say;
So unrecorded did it slip away,
    So blind was I to see and to foresee,
    So dull to mark the budding of my tree
That would not blossom yet for many a May.
If only I could recollect it, such
    A day of days! I let it come and go
    As traceless as a thaw of bygone snow;
It seemed to mean so little, meant so much;
If only now I could recall that touch,
    First touch of hand in hand – Did one but know!

LA FIGLIA CHE PIANGE

O quam te memorem virgo...

Stand on the highest pavement of the stair –
Lean on a garden urn –
Weave, weave the sunlight in your hair –
Clasp your flowers to you with a pained surprise –
Fling them to the ground and turn
With a fugitive resentment in your eyes:
But weave, weave the sunlight in your hair.

So I would have had him leave,
So I would have had her stand and grieve,
So he would have left
As the soul leaves the body torn and bruised,
As the mind deserts the body it has used.
I should find
Some way incomparably light and deft,
Some way we both should understand,
Simple and faithless as a smile and shake of the hand.

She turned away, but with the autumn weather
Compelled my imagination many days,
Many days and many hours:
Her hair over her arms and her arms full of flowers.
And I wonder how they should have been together!
I should have lost a gesture and a pose.
Sometimes these cogitations still amaze
The troubled midnight and the noon's repose.

VILLANELLE

It is the pain, it is the pain, endures.
Your chemic beauty burned my muscles through.
Poise of my hands reminded me of yours.

What later purge from this deep toxin cures?
What kindness now could the old salve renew?
It is the pain, it is the pain, endures.

The infection slept (custom or change inures)
And when pain's secondary phase was due
Poise of my hands reminded me of yours.

How safe I felt, whom memory assures,
Rich that your grace safely by heart I knew.
It is the pain, it is the pain, endures.

My stare drank deep beauty that still allures.
My heart pumps yet the poison draught of you.
Poise of my hands reminded me of yours.

You are still kind whom the same shape immures.
Kind and beyond adieu. We miss our cue.
It is the pain, it is the pain, endures.
Poise of my hands reminded me of yours.

WILLIAM EMPSON (1906–1984)   209

FAREWELL! THOU ART TOO DEAR

Farewell! thou art too dear for my possessing,
And like enough thou knowst thy estimate,
The Charter of thy worth gives thee releasing:
My bonds in thee are all determinate.
For how do I hold thee but by thy granting,
And for that riches where is my deserving?
The cause of this fair gift in me is wanting,
And so my patent back again is swerving.
Thy self thou gav'st, thy own worth then not
        knowing,
Or me to whom thou gav'st it, else mistaking,
So thy great gift upon misprision growing,
Comes home again, on better judgement making.
    Thus have I had thee as a dream doth flatter,
    In sleep a King, but waking no such matter.

INSTEAD OF WISDOM

Instead of wisdom – experience, a flat,
Unsatisfying drink.
And there was youth – like the Sunday prayer ...
Could I ever forget it?

So many deserted roads walked
With him who was not dear to me,
So many bows I made in church
For him, who loved me ...

I've become the most forgetful of all the forgetful,
Quietly the years sail by.
Those unkissed lips, unsmiling eyes
Will never return to me.

ANNA AKHMATOVA (1889–1966),   211
TRANS. JUDITH HEMSCHEMEYER

LAST LOVE

Love at the closing of our days
is apprehensive and very tender.
Glow brighter, brighter, farewell rays
of one last love in its evening splendour.

Blue shade takes half the world away:
through western clouds alone some light is slanted.
O tarry, O tarry, declining day,
enchantment, let me stay enchanted.

The blood runs thinner, yet the heart
remains as ever deep and tender.
O last belated love, thou art
a blend of joy and of hopeless surrender.

212   FYODOR TYUTCHEV (1803–1873),
      TRANS. VLADIMIR NABOKOV (1899–1977)

SONG

Sweetest love, I do not go
   For weariness of thee,
Nor in hope the world can show
   A fitter love for me;
     But since that I
Must die at last, 'tis best
To use myself in jest
   Thus by fained deaths to die.

Yesternight the sun went hence,
   And yet is here today,
He hath no desire nor sense,
   Nor half so short a way:
     Then fear not me,
But believe that I shall make
Speedier journeys, since I take
   More wings and spurs than he.

O how feeble is man's power,
    That if good fortune fall,
Cannot add another hour,
    Nor a lost hour recall!
        But come bad chance,
And we join to it our strength,
And we teach it art and length,
    Itself o'er us to advance.

When thou sigh'st, thou sigh'st not wind,
    But sigh'st my soul away,
When thou weep'st, unkindly kind,
    My life's blood doth decay.
        It cannot be
That thou lov'st me, as thou say'st,
If in thine my life thou waste,
    Thou art the best of me.

Let not thy divining heart
    Forethink me any ill,
Destiny may take thy part,
    And may thy fears fulfil;
        But think that we
Are but turned aside to sleep;
They who one another keep
    Alive, ne'er parted be.

SINCE THERE'S NO HELP

Since there's no help, come let us kiss and part –
Nay, I have done, you get no more of me;
And I am glad, yea, glad with all my heart,
That thus so cleanly I myself can free.
Shake hands for ever, cancel all our vows,
And when we meet at any time again,
Be it not seen in either of our brows
That we one jot of former love retain.
Now at the last gasp of Love's latest breath,
When, his pulse failing, Passion speechless lies,
When Faith is kneeling by his bed of death,
And Innocence is closing up his eyes,
  – Now if thou would'st, when all have given him over,
  From death to life thou might'st him yet recover.

THE EXPIRATION

So, so, break off this last lamenting kiss,
    Which sucks two souls, and vapours Both away,
Turn thou ghost that way, and let me turn this,
    And let our selves benight our happiest day,
We ask'd none leave to love; nor will we owe
    Any, so cheap a death, as saying, Go;

Go; and if that word have not quite kill'd thee,
    Ease me with death, by bidding me go too.
Oh, if it have, let my word work on me,
    And a just office on a murderer do.
Except it be too late, to kill me so,
    Being double dead, going, and bidding, go.

THE EXEQUY

Accept, thou shrine of my dead Saint!
Instead of dirges this complaint;
And for sweet flowers to crown thy hearse,
Receive a strew of weeping verse
From thy griev'd friend, whom thou might'st see
Quite melted into tears for thee.
  Dear loss! since thy untimely fate
My task hath been to meditate
On thee, on thee: thou art the book,
The library whereon I look
Though almost blind. For thee (lov'd clay!)
I languish out, not live the day,
Using no other exercise
But what I practise with mine eyes.
By which wet glasses I find out
How lazily time creeps about
To one that mourns: this, only this
My exercise and bus'ness is:
So I compute the weary hours
With sighs dissolved into showers.
  Nor wonder if my time go thus
Backward and most preposterous;
Thou hast benighted me. Thy set
This eve of blackness did beget,

Who wast my day, (though overcast
Before thou had'st thy noon-tide passed)
And I remember must in tears,
Thou scarce had'st seen so many years
As day tells hours. By thy clear sun
My love and fortune first did run;
But thou wilt never more appear
Folded within my hemisphere:
Since both thy light and motion
Like a fled star is fall'n and gone;
And twixt me and my soul's dear wish
The earth now interposed is,
With such a strange eclipse doth make
As ne'er was read in almanake.

   I could allow thee for a time
To darken me and my sad clime,
Were it a month, a year, or ten,
I would thy exile live till then;
And all that space my mirth adjourn
So thou wouldst promise to return;
And putting off thy ashy shroud
At length disperse this sorrow's cloud.

   But woe is me! the longest date
Too narrow is to calculate
These empty hopes. Never shall I
Be so much blest, as to descry

A glimpse of thee, till that day come
Which shall the earth to cinders doom,
And a fierce fever must calcine
The body of this world, like thine
(My Little World!). That fit of fire
Once off, our bodies shall aspire
To our souls' bliss: then we shall rise,
And view ourselves with clearer eyes
In that calm region, where no night
Can hide us from each other's sight.

    Meantime, thou hast her earth: much good
May my harm do thee. Since it stood
With Heaven's will I might not call
Her longer mine, I give thee all
My short-liv'd right and interest
In her, whom living I lov'd best:
With a most free and bounteous grief,
I give thee what I could not keep.
Be kind to her, and prithee look
Thou write into thy Doomsday book
Each parcel of this rarity
Which in thy casket shrin'd doth lie:
See that thou make thy reck'ning straight,
And yield her back again by weight;
For thou must audit on thy trust
Each grain and atom of this dust:

As thou wilt answer Him, that lent,
Not gave thee, my dear monument.
    So close the ground, and 'bout her shade
Black curtains draw, my bride is laid.
    Sleep on (my love!) in thy cold bed
Never to be disquieted,
My last good night! Thou wilt not wake
Till I thy fate shall overtake:
Till age, or grief, or sickness must
Marry my body to that dust
It so much loves; and fill the room
My heart keeps empty in thy tomb.
Stay for me there; I will not fail
To meet thee in that hollow vale.
And think not much of my delay;
I am already on the way,
And follow thee with all the speed
Desire can make, or sorrows breed.
Each minute is a short degree
And ev'ry hour a step towards thee.
At night when I betake to rest,
Next morn I rise nearer my west
Of life, almost by eight hours' sail,
Than when sleep breath'd his drowsy gale.

Thus from the sun my bottom steers,
And my days' compass downward bears.
Nor labour I to stem the tide,
Through which to thee I swiftly glide.

'Tis true; with shame and grief I yield,
Thou, like the van, first took'st the field,
And gotten hast the victory
In thus adventuring to die
Before me; whose more years might crave
A just precedence in the grave.
But hark! My pulse, like a soft drum
Beats my approach, tells thee I come;
And slow howe'er my marches be,
I shall at last sit down by thee.

The thought of this bids me go on,
And wait my dissolution
With hope and comfort. Dear! (forgive
The crime) I am content to live
Divided, with but half a heart,
Till we shall meet and never part.

HENRY KING (1592–1669)   221

THE LOST MISTRESS

All's over, then: does truth sound bitter
    As one at first believes?
Hark, 'tis the sparrows' good-night twitter
    About your cottage eaves!

And the leaf-buds on the vine are woolly,
    I noticed that, today;
One day more bursts them open fully
    – You know the red turns grey.

Tomorrow we meet the same then, dearest?
    May I take your hand in mine?
Mere friends are we, – well, friends the merest
    Keep much that I resign:

For each glance of the eye so bright and black,
    Though I keep with heart's endeavour, –
Your voice, when you wish the snowdrops back,
    Though it stay in my soul for ever! –

Yet I will but say what mere friends say,
    Or only a thought stronger;
I will hold your hand but as long as all may,
    Or so very little longer!

THE GOING

Why did you give no hint that night
That quickly after the morrow's dawn,
And calmly, as if indifferent quite,
You would close your term here, up and be gone
      Where I could not follow
      With wing of swallow
To gain one glimpse of you ever anon!

      Never to bid good-bye,
      Or lip me the softest call,
Or utter a wish for a word, while I
Saw morning harden upon the wall,
      Unmoved, unknowing
      That your great going
Had place that moment, and altered all.

Why do you make me leave the house
And think for a breath it is you I see
At the end of the alley of bending boughs
Where so often at dusk you used to be;
      Till in darkening dankness
      The yawning blankness
Of the perspective sickens me!

You were she who abode
By those red-veined rocks far West.
You were the swan-necked one who rode
Along the beetling Beeny Crest,
        And, reining nigh me,
        Would muse and eye me,
While Life unrolled us its very best.

Why, then, latterly did we not speak,
Did we not think of those days long dead,
And ere your vanishing strive to seek
That time's renewal? We might have said,
        'In this bright spring weather
        We'll visit together
Those places that once we visited.'

        Well, well! All's past amend,
        Unchangeable. It must go.
I seem but a dead man held on end
To sink down soon . . . O you could not know
        That such swift fleeing
        No soul foreseeing—
Not even I—would undo me so!

LOVE PAST

REMEMBER

Remember me when I am gone away,
    Gone far away into the silent land;
    When you can no more hold me by the hand,
Nor I half turn to go, yet turning stay.
Remember me when no more day by day
    You tell me of our future that you planned:
    Only remember me; you understand
It will be late to counsel then or pray.

Yet if you should forget me for a while
    And afterwards remember, do not grieve:
    For if the darkness and corruption leave
    A vestige of the thoughts that once I had,
Better by far you should forget and smile
    Than that you should remember and be sad.

A YOUNG DEAD WOMAN

No matter who you are, you are alive: pass quickly
   Among the grasses by my humble vault:
   Don't crush the flowers where I lie unconsoled
   Listening to the climbing ant and ivy.

I think you stopped. That singing was a dove:
     it moaned.
   Oh no, don't sacrifice it on my tomb.
   To earn my favour, give it flight and freedom.
   Life is so sweet: oh, let it live, my friend.

   It was under the myrtle garland, at the door,
   On the sill of marriage I died, a virgin wife,
So near – already far from him I used to love.

   So my eyes closed against the happy light.
   And now I stay – alas, for evermore –
With Erebus deaf to prayers, in the embrace of Night.

228   JOSÉ-MARIA DE HEREDIA (1842–1905),
      TRANS. ALISTAIR ELLIOT

AN EXCHANGE OF FEELINGS

In the old park, deserted in the frost,
A while ago two shapes came drifting past.

Their eyes have died, their lips become so weak
That you can hardly hear a word they speak.

In the old park, deserted in the frost,
A ghost was reminiscing to a ghost.

– Can you recall our ecstasy of long ago?
– Why stir the memory? Why do you want to know?

– Does your heart beat at just my name, as ever?
Do you still see my spirit in your dreams? – No. Never.

– O lovely days of speechless happiness
When our mouths met! – Speechless? Perhaps it was.

– How blue the sky was and what hopes we had!
– Hope ran away to the black sky, defeated.

So they walk on in the self-seeding grass
With only night to hear them as they pass.

PAUL VERLAINE (1844–1896),   229
TRANS. ALISTAIR ELLIOT

From ANACTORIA

Yea, thou shalt be forgotten like spilt wine,
Except these kisses of my lips on thine
Brand them with immortality; but me –
Men shall not see bright fire nor hear the sea,
Nor mix their hearts with music, nor behold
Cast forth of heaven, with feet of awful gold
And plumeless wings that make the bright air blind,
Lightning, with thunder for a hound behind
Hunting through fields unfurrowed and unsown,
But in the light and laughter, in the moan
And music, and in grasp of lip and hand
And shudder of water that makes felt on land
The immeasurable tremor of all the sea,
Memories shall mix and metaphors of me.

AFTER DEATH

The curtains were half drawn, the floor was swept
   And strewn with rushes, rosemary and may
Lay thick upon the bed on which I lay,
Where through the lattice ivy-shadows crept.
He leaned above me, thinking that I slept
   And could not hear him; but I heard him say,
   'Poor child, poor child': and as he turned away
Came a deep silence, and I knew he wept.
He did not touch the shroud, or raise the fold
   That hid my face, or take my hand in his,
     Or ruffle the smooth pillows for my head:
     He did not love me living; but once dead
   He pitied me; and very sweet it is
To know he still is warm though I am cold.

ENOUGH

Enough, Catullus, of this silly whining;
What you can see is lost, write off as lost.
Not long ago the sun was always shining,
And, loved as no girl ever will be loved,
She led the way and you went dancing after.
Those were the days of lovers' games and laughter
When anything you wanted she approved;
That was a time when the sun really shone.
But now she's cold, you too must learn to cool;
Weak though you are, stop groping for what's gone,
Stop whimpering, and be stoically resigned.
Goodbye, my girl. Catullus from now on
Is adamant: he has made up his mind:
He won't beg for your favour like a bone.
You'll feel the cold, though, you damned bitch, when men
Leave *you* alone. What life will you have then?
Who'll visit you? Who'll think you beautiful? Who'll
Be loved by you? Parade you as his own?
Whom will you kiss and nibble then?
                                        Oh fool,
Catullus, stop this, stand firm, become stone.

MEMORY OF LOVE

Memory of love, you are painful!
I must sing and burn in your smoke,
But for others – you're just a flame
To warm a cooling soul.

To warm a sated body,
They needed my tears ...
For this, Lord, I sang,
For this I received love's communion!

Let me drink some kind of poison
That will make me mute,
And turn my infamous fame
Into radiant oblivion.

ANNA AKHMATOVA (1889–1966),   233
TRANSLATED JUDITH HEMSCHEMEYER

I, BEING BORN A WOMAN

I, being born a woman and distressed
By all the needs and notions of my kind,
Am urged by your propinquity to find
Your person fair, and feel a certain zest
To bear your body's weight upon my breast:
So subtly is the fume of life designed,
To clarify the pulse and cloud the mind,
And leave me once again undone, possessed.
Think not for this, however, the poor treason
Of my stout blood against my staggering brain,
I shall remember you with love, or season
My scorn with pity, – let me make it plain:
I find this frenzy insufficient reason
For conversation when we meet again.

BODY, REMEMBER ...

Body, remember not only how much you were loved,
not only the beds on which you lay,
but also those desires for you
that glowed plainly in the eyes,
and trembled in the voice – and some
chance obstacle made futile.
Now that all of them belong to the past,
it almost seems as if you had yielded
to those desires – how they glowed,
remember, in the eyes gazing at you;
how they trembled in the voice, for you, remember,
 body.

C. P. CAVAFY (1863–1933),
TRANS. RAE DALVEN

ONE NIGHT

The room was poor and squalid,
hidden above the dubious tavern.
From the window you could see the alley
filthy and narrow. From below
came the voices of some workmen
playing cards and carousing.

And there on the much-used, lowly bed
I had the body of love, I had the lips,
the voluptuous and rosy lips of ecstasy —
rosy lips of such ecstasy, that even now
as I write, after so many years!
in my solitary house, I am drunk again.

C. P. CAVAFY (1863–1933),
TRANS. RAE DALVEN

LOST LOVE

His eyes are quickened so with grief,
He can watch a grass or leaf
Every instant grow; he can
Clearly through a flint wall see,
Or watch the startled spirit flee
From the throat of a dead man.
  Across two counties he can hear
And catch your words before you speak.
The woodlouse or the maggot's weak
Clamour rings in his sad ear,
And noise so slight it would surpass
Credence – drinking sound of grass,
Worm talk, clashing jaws of moth
Chumbling holes in cloth;
The groan of ants who undertake
Gigantic loads for honour's sake
(Their sinews creak, their breath comes thin);
Whir of spiders when they spin,
And minute whispering, mumbling, sighs
Of idle grubs and flies.
  This man is quicked so with grief,
He wanders god-like or like thief
Inside and out, below, above,
Without relief seeking lost love.

ROBERT GRAVES (1895–1985)   237

WHITE HELIOTROPE

The feverish room and that white bed,
The tumbled skirts upon a chair,
The novel flung half-open where
Hat, hair-pins, puffs, and paints, are spread;

The mirror that has sucked your face
Into its secret deep of deeps,
And there mysteriously keeps
Forgotten memories of grace;

And you, half dressed and half awake,
Your slant eyes strangely watching me,
And I, who watch you drowsily,
With eyes that, having slept not, ache;

This (need one dread? nay, dare one hope?)
Will rise, a ghost of memory, if
Ever again my handkerchief
Is scented with White Heliotrope.

THE VOICE

Woman much missed, how you call to me, call to me,
Saying that now you are not as you were
When you had changed from the one who was all to me,
But as at first, when our day was fair.

Can it be you that I hear? Let me view you, then,
Standing as when I drew near to the town
Where you would wait for me: yes, as I knew you then,
Even to the original air-blue gown!

Or is it only the breeze, in its listlessness
Travelling across the wet mead to me here,
You being ever consigned to existlessness,
Heard no more again far or near?

   Thus I: faltering forward,
   Leaves around me falling,
Wind oozing thin through the thorn from northward,
   And the woman calling.

THOMAS HARDY (1840–1928)   239

AFTER A JOURNEY

Hereto I come to view a voiceless ghost;
    Whither, O whither will its whim now draw me?
Up the cliff, down, till I'm lonely, lost,
    And the unseen waters' ejaculations awe me.
Where you will next be there's no knowing,
    Facing round about me everywhere,
      With your nut-coloured hair,
And grey eyes, and rose-flush coming and going.

Yes: I have re-entered your olden haunts at last;
    Through the years, through the dead scenes I have
      tracked you;
What have you now found to say of our past –
    Scanned across the dark space wherein I have lacked
      you?
Summer gave us sweets, but autumn wrought division?
    Things were not lastly as firstly well
      With us twain, you tell?
But all's closed now, despite Time's derision.

I see what you are doing: you are leading me on
    To the spots we knew when we haunted here
        together,
The waterfall, above which the mist-bow shone
    At the then fair hour in the then fair weather,
And the cave just under, with a voice still so hollow
    That it seems to call out to me from forty years ago,
        When you were all aglow,
And not the thin ghost that I now fraily follow!

Ignorant of what there is flitting here to see,
    The waked birds preen and the seals flop lazily;
Soon you will have, Dear, to vanish from me,
    For the stars close their shutters and the dawn
        whitens hazily.
Trust me, I mind not, though Life lours,
    The bringing me here; nay, bring me here again!
        I am just the same as when
Our days were a joy, and our paths through flowers.

THE GHOST

'Who knocks?' 'I, who was beautiful,
　　Beyond all dreams to restore,
I, from the roots of the dark thorn am hither.
　　And knock on the door.'

'Who speaks?' 'I – once was my speech
　　Sweet as the bird's on the air,
When echo lurks by the waters to heed;
　　'Tis I speak thee fair.'

'Dark is the hour!' 'Ay, and cold.'
　　'Lone is my house.' 'Ah, but mine?'
'Sight, touch, lips, eyes yearned in vain.'
　　'Long dead these to thine . . .'

Silence. Still faint on the porch
　　Brake the flames of the stars.
In gloom groped a hope-wearied hand
　　Over keys, bolts, and bars.

A face peered. All the grey night
　　In chaos of vacancy shone;
Nought but vast sorrow was there –
　　The sweet cheat gone.

MUSIC

Music, when soft voices die,
Vibrates in the memory –
Odours, when sweet violets sicken,
Live within the sense they quicken.
Rose leaves, when the rose is dead,
Are heaped for the belovèd's bed;
And so thy thoughts, when thou art gone,
Love itself shall slumber on.

WHAT LIPS MY LIPS HAVE KISSED

What lips my lips have kissed, and where, and why,
I have forgotten, and what arms have lain
Under my head till morning; but the rain
Is full of ghosts tonight, that tap and sigh
Upon the glass and listen for reply,
And in my heart there stirs a quiet pain
For unremembered lads that not again
Will turn to me at midnight with a cry.
Thus in the winter stands the lonely tree,
Nor knows what birds have vanished one by one,
Yet knows its boughs more silent than before:
I cannot say what loves have come and gone;
I only know that summer sang in me
A little while, that in me sings no more.

WHEN YOU ARE OLD

When you are old and grey and full of sleep,
And nodding by the fire, take down this book,
And slowly read, and dream of the soft look
Your eyes had once, and of their shadows deep;

How many loved your moments of glad grace,
And loved your beauty with love false or true,
But one man loved the pilgrim soul in you,
And loved the sorrows of your changing face;

And bending down beside the glowing bars,
Murmur, a little sadly, how Love fled
And paced upon the mountains overhead
And hid his face amid a crowd of stars.

JENNY KISS'D ME

Jenny kiss'd me when we met,
    Jumping from the chair she sat in;
Time, you thief, who love to get
    Sweets into your list, put that in!
Say I'm weary, say I'm sad,
    Say that health and wealth have miss'd me,
Say I'm growing old, but add,
       Jenny kiss'd me.

ACKNOWLEDGMENTS

Thanks are due to the following copyright holders for permission to reprint poems in this volume:

Aitken, Stone & Wylie Ltd. for Charles Baudelaire, tr. Roy Campbell, 'The Jewels'.
Basic Books Inc., for Andrei Voznesensky, tr. Richard Wilbur, 'Dead Still'.
Bloodaxe Books Ltd., for Alistair Elliot's translations of La Fontaine, 'Thyrsis And Amaranta', Ronsard, 'Sonnet For Helen', Leconte de Lisle, 'The Palanquin', Bellay, 'To Venus', Baudelaire, 'She Is Not Satisfied', Verlaine, 'Nevermore', 'An Exchange Of Feelings', Hérédia, 'A Young Dead Woman', Mallarmé, 'Another Fan'.
Canongate Press, Edinburgh, and Zephyr Press, Boston, for Anna Akhmatova, tr. Judith Hemschemeyer, 'The Lord Is Not', 'To The Beloved', 'I Will Leave Your White House', 'He Whispers', 'Ah, You Thought', 'Instead of Wisdom', 'Memory Of Love'.
Doubleday and Co., Inc., for Wên T'ing-yün, tr. William R. Schultz, 'In The Moonlit Chamber', 'A Song of Chang Ching-yūan Picking Lotus Flowers', tr. Li Shang-Yin, tr. Eugene Eoyang and Irving Y. Lo, 'Willow'.
Farrar, Straus & Giroux, Inc., for John Berryman,

Company, Inc., for Emily Dickinson, 'Love Thou Art High', 'Love Is That Later Thing', 'The Love A Life'.
David Higham Associates, for Apollinaire, tr. Quentin Stevenson, 'The Mirabeau Bridge'.
Henry Holt & Company, Inc., for Robert Frost, 'He Would Declare'.
Macmillan Publishing Company, for W. B. Yeats, 'Lullaby', 'A Drinking Song', 'The Folly Of Being Comforted', 'When You Are Old'.
Alfred A. Knopf Inc., for Elinor Wylie, 'Wild Peaches'; Arthur Waley, tr., 'Plucking The Rushes'.
Mrs Mary Martin, for Paulinus, 'I, Through All Chances' and Venantius Fortunatus, 'To The Lady Radegund', tr. Helen Waddell.
James Michie for his translation of Horace, 'The Young Bloods'.
The Estate of Vladimir Nabokov for Nabokov's translation of Fyodor Tyutchev, 'Last Love'.
New Directions Publishing Corporation, for Izumi Shikibu, tr. Jane Hirshfield and Mariko Aratani, 'Come Quickly'; Li Po, tr. Ezra Pound, 'The River-Merchant's Wife: A Letter'; William Carlos Williams, 'Sweep The House Clean'.
Oxford University Press, Inc., for Robert Graves, 'Never Such Love', 'Problems Of Gender', 'Symptoms Of Love', 'The Portrait', 'Conjunction', 'The Thieves', 'She Tells Her Love While Half Asleep', 'Friday Night',

INDEX OF FIRST LINES

255